WHEN
THE MINISTER
IS A
WOMAN

WHEN THE MINISTER IS A *Woman*

Elsie Gibson

HOLT, RINEHART AND WINSTON

New York   Chicago   San Francisco

ACKNOWLEDGMENTS

I am grateful to the 270 ordained women, mentioned by name in the second Appendix, whose shared experience made this book possible. But I would also like to thank women seminary students and recent graduates who have given their own special perspective to this work as well as many unordained women who, having spent their lives in the service of the church, contributed insight through correspondence. Denominational leaders, too, have been generous in answering questions; this has made it possible to learn of trends through material not yet available in published form.

My special thanks for permission to read theses goes to: Oberlin College Library for "A Study of Important Factors Involved in the Placement and Service of Ordained Women Ministers in Local Protestant Churches" (1948) by the Reverend Mrs. Mary H. Candy; Berkeley Baptist Divinity School and the Reverend Miss Elaine Marsh for "The Leadership of Women in the Christian Church" (1946); Lancaster Theological Seminary for "The Status of Women in the Ministry with Reference to Ordination" (1959) by the Reverend Mrs. Ruthanne K. Cochran; and Mrs. Suzanne Helene Dettmer for her study, "Some Fac-

47371

v

tors Pertaining to the Work of Women Chaplains in Hospitals," done for her B. D. degree at Union Theological Seminary (1967).

I deeply appreciate the constant, courteous help of librarians at Hartford Theological Seminary, the editorial assistance of Joseph Cunneen, and the sense of humor and encouragement of Royal Gibson, my husband.

E. G.

March, 1970

CONTENTS

Contents

The Sacraments
By What Authority?
What Does Ordination Accomplish?

PREFACE

It is no new thing for a woman to be a mystery to a man, but nowhere does the mystery seem more impenetrable than when a woman brings her femininity (or lack of it) into traditionally masculine professions. Why does she want to do this? Dark Freudian interpretations are frequently given without really explaining anything. The women who succeed in entering professional male preserves are apt to encounter hostility, amused tolerance, or acceptance, but seldom genuine awareness of why they are there. Women doctors, journalists and scientists, however, have at least won grudging acknowledgment, as a predictable element in their various fields of endeavor, but women ministers are apparently not yet credible to the general public.

Christians assume that God can speak; does he never speak to women? In *Consultation on Church Union*, prepared by representatives of nine Protestant denominations hoping for merger, it is stated: "God calls men to the ministry of word and sacrament and gives them the gifts needed to carry out their calling." [1] The words are crystal clear to men; to women, they are about as opaque as words can be. What does "men" mean: human beings or adult males? Does the word exclude women from the ministry of word and sacrament, the traditional view of Catholic, Orthodox and Episcopal Churches,[2] or does it include them, as more than eighty Protestant bodies believe? [3] The place of men in the church is assured; the place of women is an enigma.

My appreciation of the magnitude and complexity of difficulties confronting women who feel called to the ministry came to a focus during the preparation of an article, "Protestant Women in Religion," which appeared in the Jesuit quarterly *Review for Religious*, November 1967. In a desire to make the article a true reflection of Protestant experience I had sent out a simple questionnaire to about 280 ordained women, to which approximately 160 replied. The questionnaire (Appendix 1) had not been designed to produce sociological data which could be statistically measured; its purpose was to facilitate communication between Catholic and Protestant women engaged in professional Christian work. The discoveries I made, therefore, were thought-provoking rather than conclusive. They led to the writing of this book, to which, through correspondence and interview, 270 ordained women have contributed, some minimally, some extensively.

My purpose here is to show the variety of ministries to which women have been ordained and how professional status has helped them. But these ministries do not exist in a vacuum; they have a history and they present problems. For that reason, returns from the questionnaire are set within the framework of woman's background in the church and present ecclesiastical practice in her regard (Chapter 1) and a highly tentative surmise regarding future trends if the ordination of women becomes widespread (Chapter 6).

The practical problems presented by female clergy are immense and diverse. No one knows this better than bishops, superintendents and presidents of churches. They are caught between the pleas of women who want to serve and churches that are afraid of innovation. I have myself been in the middle of this situation for a long time because I am an ordained minister, and because my husband has been engaged, for more than twenty years, in helping churches to find ministers and ministers to find churches.

When he first mentioned that women were hard to place, I was surprised because I had encountered no prejudice in seminary from faculty or students. Moreover, I had given supply and interim service to churches whose members had told me I was the first woman to occupy their pulpits and I had detected no anti-feminine bias in the remark. "That was because they knew you," my husband replied. "When churches know a woman, they are more likely to accept her. The problem stems from their unwillingness to meet her as a potential candidate." Half a dozen or more respondents from different denominations were told the same thing. One said that she had been sent by her conference minister to look over two parishes, neither of which wanted a woman minister. He did not tell the churches she was coming (an unusual procedure) but gave her the addresses of deacons. When the members had heard her preach and had become acquainted with her, she was forced to choose between the congregations; both wanted her as pastor.

In sending out my questionnaires, I felt it important to request information as to age and marital status, despite the fact that most women ministers do not consider the latter a prime element in the discussion of their work. However, although few denominational officials today would want to argue that sex is destiny, the reality of the situation is that biological and sociological factors are not (and cannot be) ignored when women are considered for employment. Local churches do not live in a rarefied spiritual atmosphere; they are social bodies with keen awareness that the novelty of a woman in the pulpit will have repercussions on both public and church opinion.

We should not be too surprised, then, if women presenting themselves before ecclesiastical councils to be examined regarding their suitability for ordination are asked questions of a kind never put to men: "Don't you want to get married sometime? Well, if you do, what about your husband and his work?" As one respondent commented:

> The Council seemed much more concerned about my being a woman than about my theological views. The main line of questioning had to do with whether or not I expected to have children; would I be able to keep my husband satisfied and approving; what would I say to St. Paul about women speaking in church?

Another was disappointed that so little emphasis was placed "on substantive issues like theology, church polity, style of ministry." Interest seemed to center about her ideas of "women in the ministry."

Age grouping is also significant. Obviously, it makes a great deal of difference whether a woman had her theological training forty years ago or has just completed studies. Since it is usually harder for her to obtain her first appointment and since it is unlikely she will be ordained until she is established at some post, she may be a little older than men at the time of ordination. In order to have a balanced response, which would include adequate expression from young women, I have corresponded with well over a dozen girls who are now in seminary or who, having just graduated, are looking toward their professional careers. Because they have not yet been ordained however, they are not included in the tables that follow nor in Appendix 2, where respondents are listed.

AGE	MARITAL STATUS				
	Single	*Married*	*Widowed*	*Divorced*	*Total*
Under 40	27	26		2	55
40–60	46	58	11	6	121
Past 60	42	21	24	3	90
Undesignated		4			4
TOTAL	115	109	35	11	270

Because my interest in writing the article which prompted this book had been ecumenical, most of the questionnaires went first to women in churches engaged in the Consultation on Church Union or participating as observers. Churches actually in the Consultation are starred below. In widening the study, however, I sought the help of women in Pentecostal and Unitarian-Universalist Churches along with others more difficult to classify. Distribution is as follows:

Advent Christian	2	Full Gospel	2
African Methodist		Presbyterian U.S.*	5
Episcopal *	2	Salvation Army	8
American Baptist	20	Spiritualist	1
Assemblies of God	4	Unitarian-Universalist	13
Christian (Disciples of		United Church of Canada	1
Christ) *	16	United Church of Christ *	104
Church of the Living God	1	United Methodist *	40
Church of the Nazarene	3	United Presbyterian	
Community	1	U.S.A.*	34
Free Methodist	1	Wesleyan Church	6
Friends	6		

The United Church of Christ, a merger of the former Congregational-Christian Churches and the Evangelical and Reformed Church, is now well into its second decade of existence. Respondents come from both backgrounds. In 1968, the Evangelical United Brethren Church and the Methodist Church became one United Methodist body.

Four or five respondents come from the E. U. B. background. The Wesleyan Church came into being in 1968, also, through the merger of the Wesleyan Methodist and Pilgrim Holiness Churches. All respondents in that grouping are from the former body. The Salvation Army and Friends do not speak of ordination. Quakers believe that only God can ordain; the church "records." The Salvation Army "commissions" its officers, but the process followed in these groups is similar to that of ordination and equal status is given to men and women.

Ordained women are not listed separately by any denomination, as far as I know, nor should they be; and no effort was made to cull their names from the many thousand clergy listed by various churches. My first thought had been to confine the inquiry to the United States but as names, coming to me from many sources, included several from Canada, the provinces represented are listed below in alphabetical order among the states. The table does not necessarily indicate that the states represented by the majority of respondents are those with the most women clergy, but a few general observations may be made. Where there is Free Church strength, as in old Congregational New England, there will be women ministers, since Free Churches have been ordaining them for many years. Women ministers also find acceptance in strongly rural areas that cannot support men with families and where, as a consequence, there are more empty pulpits. In addition, women are frequently found on multiple staffs in city churches. It seems probable that female clergy are distributed over all of the United States.

Alabama	1	District of Columbia	2
Arkansas	1	Florida	3
California	24	Georgia	4
Colorado	2	Idaho	1
Connecticut	23	Illinois	11

Indiana	14	North Carolina	1
Iowa	4	Ohio	16
Kansas	1	Ontario	1
Kentucky	4	Oregon	1
Maine	14	Pennsylvania	12
Manitoba	1	Saskatchewan	1
Maryland	5	South Dakota	1
Massachusetts	22	Tennessee	2
Michigan	19	Texas	5
Minnesota	8	Utah	1
Missouri	8	Vermont	10
Nebraska	3	Virginia	3
New Hampshire	5	Washington	1
New Jersey	4	West Virginia	2
New York	24	Wisconsin	5

The next table will show the work being done by respondents. Where a woman carries more than one responsibility she is included where she seems to be giving the most time. For example, if she is teaching religion in a college, but supplying churches, I have listed her with teachers. If she is a minister's wife, and doing only interim preaching, the first category is chosen. If she is a full-time Minister of Christian Education, but also a minister's wife, she is included with Ministers of Christian Education. Nearly all of the retired women are doing some writing and speaking, but if they are giving full time to any form of ministry, even without remuneration, they are classified under that ministry.

Pastors	81
Associate pastors	15
Assistant pastors	16
Ministers of Christian Education	18
Directors of Christian Education	3
Evangelists	4
In mission work	3
In denominational work	16

Chaplains: in educational institutions   3
            in hospitals   4
            in retirement homes   2
            in correctional institutions   1
In counseling work   2
Teachers: in seminary   5
           in college   8
           in private school   1
           in public school   3
Editors and writers   4
Other specialized ministries   9
Ministers' wives   20
Graduate students
   (ordained and back in school)   6
Retired   40
Limited employment due to ill health   3
Changing form of ministry
   and temporarily unemployed   3

Many churches today are conducting an intensive study of ministry in all its forms. Some of those that do not now ordain women have committees or sub-committees investigating the subject.

1.

The Developing Ministry of Women

The ministry of women cannot be considered apart from the total mission of the church, but today the mission of the church is itself problematic. Has this institution a divine origin? If it has, is God still taking the initiative in its life, or do human leaders, tracing what appears to be a thread of redemptive purpose through history, chart its course? To pose the question with special reference to the ordained ministry: does God call individuals and bestow gifts upon them, trusting the church to discern and ordain those thus endowed, or does the church choose and recruit clergy, hopefully petitioning God to empower them? If we narrow the question still further to the place of women in the church, we might ask: does God call women to share the ministry with men, or do some women simply have vivid imaginations regarding their destiny?

Two simplistic answers must, I think, be avoided: first, dismissing the idea of divine call as outmoded supernaturalism and, second, assuming that a woman's sexual function precludes her participation in public life. With regard to the first, are we sufficiently advanced in scientific knowledge to delimit the natural in this way? Are there no longer any mysteries? The fact that we are unable to locate and assess the action of any supreme being on human minds and society does not in itself establish that there is no such presence and power operative in the world. If religion must be modest about its revelations, is it not equally true that the behavioral sciences should avoid dogmatism about the absence of revelation?

On the second count, it seems reasonable to suppose that the biological difference between men and women will have some effect upon the development of their work in the world, but it is by no means clear that certain blanket restrictions, based on sex, can be stretched over half the human race. Female ministry cannot *ipso facto* be limited to certain areas on the basis of a foregone conclusion.

Neither men nor women are to blame for history; the main thing now is to cooperate in progress. Part of the problem for the church is that so few women have had either the training or the opportunity to become theologically articulate. While some men have honestly tried to represent female concerns at conciliar levels, women themselves have often been denied this privilege. A few years ago I heard a Roman Catholic priest-sociologist say he wished he knew what place women wanted in the church so that he could help them reach it; there are doubtless many other men who feel the same way. They are put off, on the one hand, by the militancy of women about their rights, and on the other, by their silence in regard to their deepest desires.

Communication is needed, but where the meaning of ministry is concerned, this is not usually easy. Mission is not found lying on the surface of life; it has to be searched out, partly through acceptance of ourselves as we are, partly through interaction with our own and the opposite sex, partly through estimation of our resources in the light of world need, and partly through more or less conscious relationship with God. The discernment of potential ministries calls for a profound sharing among men and women of their hopes and fears, willingness to speak honestly in confidence and respect, sustained efforts to comprehend their mutual dialogue with that mysterious challenger of human thought, and an avoidance of talking past flesh-and-blood persons to idealized versions of what the opposite sex ought to do and say.

In this quest it is necessary to consider the Bible, not in proof-text fashion with a view to finding support for preconceived notions, but with a genuine wish to be enlightened by the Holy Spirit. Humility is required on the part of both men and women if they are to discover the underlying meaning that travels through the many nuances of psychological and sociological conditioning.

JESUS' ATTITUDE TOWARD WOMEN

I have, therefore, chosen six biblical passages which seem to have indirect relevance to the position and work of women in the church. The first is Mark 5:21–34.[1] Jesus has received an urgent request from a prominent Jewish leader to come to his house and heal his little daughter, who is at the point of death. As usual a large crowd is on hand to watch developments. It includes a woman whose last hope for healing a miserable hemorrhage centers in Jesus. She has no intention of speaking to him or causing the slightest delay, but tells herself that if she can touch his clothing she will be well. That touch brings instantaneous relief. Then the whole matter is taken out of her hands as Jesus whirls about with the question, "Who touched me?" The crowd is electrified. What does he mean? There is a long moment of consternation in which Peter calls his attention to the mass of people, but Jesus' eyes continue to search face after face; as they rest upon the woman, she knows that she has been singled out of the crowd and tells her story publicly. Jesus' response is, "Your faith has made you well."

It is possible to conclude that he wanted to lift her from a magical view of his healing power (if that was her idea) to a recognition of the centrality of faith. But there are two other things to note: first, he interrupts a mission of crucial importance to a man in order to help a woman; second, he is unwilling to let her go without eliciting her public confession of faith. No doubt she would have praised God with her family and friends for the rest of her life, but Jesus was not satisfied with any such hidden ministry. He permitted this with others, even taking one blind man out of town to heal him.[2] Perhaps at that time he wanted to avoid publicity, but why did he not allow the woman the same privacy? There is no easy answer to this, for his every relationship seems unique. There are women today who would welcome a hidden service but are called to that personal witness which is the core of every public mission.

The second reference (Luke 8:1–3) reveals that women, as well as men, traveled in the company of Jesus.[3] We are told that some of them contributed to the financial support of the little band, but all were listening and learning. I recently asked a seminary professor of New Testament if there was any real reason to think women were not included in the seventy persons Jesus sent to announce his coming in the towns he expected to visit.[4] After thinking a moment, he replied, "No, any reason one could adduce against it would be based on *a priori* assumptions; we simply do not know." Why should there not have been husband-wife teams in this work? No neglect of children would have resulted even if the couples were young. Family structures differed from ours. To us, father, mother and children represent the usual circle; in Jesus' time, families were large, including many adult relatives near at hand.

Children may even have accompanied their parents, as their presence is frequently noted in the New Testament.

A third point, in considering Jesus' attitude toward women, is the fact that he talked with them on questions of theology. This is especially noteworthy because then, far more than now, popular thought would have placed such matters beyond the interest and competence of women. Male disciples found this practice so astounding that the record could not have been invented. One such conversation took place between Martha and Jesus at the time of her brother Lazarus' death.[5] It was a painful situation. She and her sister, Mary, had informed Jesus (their intimate friend) when Lazarus first became ill, but he had not come. This was understandable because the political situation in nearby Jerusalem was so tense that appearing in the vicinity might have cost his life. When he finally arrived, therefore, four days after Lazarus' death, Martha, the activist of the two sisters, said forthrightly, "Lord, if you had been here, my brother would not have died. And even now I know that whatever you ask from God, God will give you." Then follows a conversation of immense significance to the Christian's faith in life after death.

The fourth chapter of John's Gospel records an even longer private theological conversation of Jesus' with a woman he was meeting for the first time, one of another race. He initiated it, and when his disciples returned, they were dumbfounded to find that he had been talking with a foreign woman who, moreover, had had a series of husbands. The woman left with a mission to her city. There is little doubt that he also had many theological conversations with Mary Magdalene and Mary of Bethany, as well as with his mother. The intellectual response of women to the teaching of Jesus is taken for granted everywhere.

Some of his teachings have become so familiar today that we fail to recognize their revolutionary character. One example of this, and my fourth reference, is his abolition of the double standard of morals. This brought dismay to the men who followed him, not because they wanted license for themselves, but because they could not see men accepting a single standard. The Sermon on the Mount (Matthew 5:27–32) sets forth Jesus' teaching with regard to adultery and divorce. Later, some Jewish leaders appeared and argued against his position but he restated it with emphasis.[6] Men and women followers face the same moral standards. Would he have differentiated as to their freedom in other matters, such as ministry? This is an open question.

The last two passages are the most important. All four Gospels make clear that women were the first witnesses of the resurrection; they were sent to give the good news to the apostles, who did not accept their report: "These words seemed to them an idle tale and they did not believe them." [7] Later, the men, too, saw the risen Lord and believed. But why should women have been the first witnesses? M. Madeline Southard, founder of the American Association of Women Ministers, makes this suggestion: had women not been the first witnesses, we should probably never have known that they were witnesses at all, because when both sexes were present, according to the custom of the day, women were usually not mentioned.[8] For example, when Paul summarizes resurrection appearances (I Corinthians 15:5–9), he omits those made to women.

In any case, the news of Jesus' triumph over death, which is the root of all Christian preaching, was first carried by women to the top authorities of the church—the apostles. Do women need a further charter for the proclamation now?

After the followers of Christ had witnessed the event referred to as his "ascension into heaven," they assembled for prolonged prayer as they had been instructed to do. Women were also present, as we find in The Acts of the Apostles 1:14.[9] After ten days of persistent prayer, the Holy Spirit descended, in order that the followers of Jesus might have power to proclaim his word and do his work.

Women received this Spirit and spoke under the same powerful influence that was moving the men.[10] Moreover, this was in fulfillment of a prophecy that included both sexes:

> And it shall come to pass afterward,
>   that I will pour out my spirit on all flesh;
> your sons and your daughters shall prophesy.
> Even upon the menservants and maidservants
>   in those days, I will pour out my spirit. (Joel 2:28ff.)

Two things of importance to the ministry of women should be noted here. First, Luke, almost certainly the author of Acts, was a close associate of Paul, whose authority is often cited when women are refused ordination. While it is possible that Luke's favorable attitude toward women indicates a basic difference to what is often regarded as a highly critical attitude on the part of Paul, it is not probable. Perhaps too little attention has been given to the friendly relations of Paul with women in the early church, described not only in Acts but in Paul's own letters.

The second and more important point is that women, in receiving the Holy Spirit, were related directly to God in the matter of their Christian lives and work. They were not made wholly dependent upon men, who would relay God's will to them. By what right, then, do men alone rule the church, thinking and speaking for it?

Some will undoubtedly say that no woman was chosen as an apostle, but the New Testament itself is silent as to the reason for this. As we have seen, there were women witnesses of the resurrection, which was a prime requirement of apostleship at the beginning. It is worth remembering, too, that no Gentiles were among the original twelve—Jesus had even stated at times that his mission was to the Jews, yet Gentiles were not ruled out of leadership in the church. Perhaps the choice of the apostles, related to the twelve tribes of Israel, may have signified continuity in the new Israel without sanctifying all the implications of the old order.

EARLY CHRISTIAN WOMEN LEADERS

The young church moved out into the Greco-Roman world very soon after the outpouring of the Holy Spirit. This does not mean that all the Christians left Jerusalem but the spotlight falls on those who left rather than those who stayed. The women in Acts are quite different personalities from those encountered in the four Gospels. Priscilla, for example, was a native of Rome. Inscriptions found in the catacombs and elsewhere identify her as the daughter of a distinguished family with high social standing. It is thought that they disowned her when she married Aquila, a Jew. Later, under persecution, the young couple left Rome and settled in Corinth, where they met Paul, who was both a Jew and a sophisticated citizen of the world with which they were familiar. The three were doubly congenial because they shared the same trade, tentmaking or leather work. At the time Paul left Corinth, the couple moved to Ephesus but remained in close touch with him.

In Ephesus, the teaching gifts of Priscilla and Aquila became apparent. While worshiping in the synagogue, as Christians often did, they heard the preaching of a brilliant young Alexandrian Jew who showed remarkable understanding of Scripture, was fervent in speaking about Jesus, but seemed never to have heard of Christian baptism. They took him home with them and shared what they had learned about Christ. Their instruction must have been thorough, for we meet the young Apollos subsequently as he travels about preaching and receives an occasional message through a New Testament letter.

The theory that Priscilla wrote the New Testament Letter to the Hebrews has been advanced by three scholars—Harnack, Harris and Peake.[11] The source of this book has always been a mystery; in the year 225, Origen said, "Who wrote the Epistle to the Hebrews, only God knows." This anonymity is so amazing that it is regarded as one of the hints suggesting female authorship.

Phoebe, another woman leader of the early church, is introduced briefly in a single sentence which stands at the beginning of the sixteenth chapter of Romans. In her capacity as deaconess of the church at Cenchreae, Paul is giving her the credentials which will insure her acceptance by the church in Rome, where she is to carry his communication; in those days postal service was available to officials only. That Phoebe was a deaconess should make her position in the church clear, but it does not. No issue has been more hotly debated through the centuries than church structure; an outsider could conclude that relative human authority is the most vital aspect of our faith. The most we can say for this woman is that she was a responsible person who could be trusted with an important mission in the church.

The same chapter sends greetings to other women: Mary, Persis, Julia, Tryphena and Tryphosa, Nereus' sister and Rufus' mother. A slight touch of humor may be intended when Paul calls Tryphena and Tryphosa "those workers in the Lord," since their names mean "dainty" and "delicate". It is interesting to speculate about Rufus' mother, whom Paul calls "mine also." Simon of Cyrene, who carried Jesus' cross after he had fallen, had a son by the name of Rufus, greeted in this same chapter as "eminent in the Lord." Is this the family with that intimate relationship to Christ?

The hair-splitting that can break out when old documents are being perused is illustrated in the seventh verse. The female Junia of the King James Version of the Bible has become the male Junias of modern translations. Apparently the Greek says "Junia," a common name for Roman girls, but it can also be a contraction of a less common man's name.[12] Because no other woman apostles are known, male translators have decided that this person belongs to them. The estimate is probably accurate, if not generous, but there is one quirk in the argument which could not fail to catch a woman's eye. Chrysostom, Doctor of the Eastern Church and Patriarch of Constantinople, who lived in the fourth century, was not troubled by a woman's presence in such august company but rather, in preaching, used it to spur the women of his generation to greater holiness, "Oh! how great is the devotion of this woman, that she should be even counted worthy of the appellation of apostle." [13]

Another leading early Christian woman about whom we have scant information is Lydia.[14] When Paul and his companions arrived at Philippi and inquired for the Jewish place of worship, they were directed to a riverside beyond the city limits. Paul spoke to a group of women gathered there and Luke tells us, "The Lord opened [Lydia's] heart to give heed to what was said." She was a well-to-do businesswoman, probably having a large home, including slaves. They were all baptized and she became hostess to the Christian group, receiving them back warmly even after they had had trouble with the authorities and spent a night in jail. It is a well known fact that the church at Philippi gladly assumed financial responsibility for Paul's work. Did Lydia's attitude as a wealthy member help to shape this policy?

Many other women are mentioned in the New Testament; their gifts vary from making clothing for the poor (Acts 9:36ff.) to prophesying. Most people would define "prophecy" as the prediction of future events, but the word has a wider connotation in the New Testament.[15] It may refer to any inspired utterance which builds up the church. Ideally, of course, this is what preaching is. Luke mentions four unmarried daughters of one family who prophesied.[16]

Although they lived in Jerusalem and were contemporaries of the women Jesus knew, they probably never met him personally, for they were Greek-Jews.[17] After his death, as the church was growing rapidly, the Greeks felt that their widows were being neglected in the relief given by the largely Jewish Christian community—not an uncommon complaint of minority groups. Righting this injustice would take so much time that the apostles could not handle it and also see to their other work, so seven men were elected to take it over. This group, set apart by prayer and the laying on of hands, included Philip, father of the four girls, and Stephen.

Not long after that, Stephen was stoned to death by a mob and Philip fled with his family to Caesarea. Paul, Luke, and others who were working together as missionaries were entertained there by Philip when they were on their way back to Jerusalem. Scholars believe that this trip, which led to Paul's long imprisonment, freed Luke to interview eyewitnesses in Palestine who could tell him about Jesus and events in the earliest church. It is quite possible that Luke includes the reference to these four women because their inspired words gave him help in this project. Whether or not this is true, however, the very least the reference could signify is that women as well as men had the gift of prophetic utterance. There had also been early precedents for female prophecy in Israel.

THROUGH THE CENTURIES

Within the biblical record itself, one can discern that deteriorating estimate of woman's place in the church that was to become more pronounced later. As Elsie Thomas Culver says, "Actually what we know concerning women's work in the churches during the first few centuries of the Christian era comes not from records of what they are permitted or expected to do, but from some theologian's speculation or some council's decision as to things they are *no longer permitted to do*." [18]

Two points may help to explain the curtailment of women's work. First, the influence of the culture, always subordinating women to men, was so pervasive that the church itself was almost inevitably affected. Christian teaching and living can only be maintained by constant re-orientation to the deeds and words of Jesus, along with an ever-recurring renewal and reformation. When Christians forget the Spirit to whom they belong, the church tends simply to reflect the dominant culture, and the age-old battle of the sexes erupts again. Women are seen as inferior beings who threaten the integrity of men, and eliminating them from ecclesiastical circles is easier than the costly search for understanding and cooperation in the work of God. Because men are physically stronger, the recognition of woman's equality depends upon male sensitivity to moral and spiritual values.

It is to the credit of men, however, both in and out of the church, that they have so often been able to recognize feminine goodness when they saw it, and to help in their search for spiritual growth. In the early centuries, virgins and widows had special opportunities for service as well as women who worked with their husbands. When political developments made it advantageous or necessary for the Empire to adopt Christianity, and the influx of the masses diluted church standards to the level of surrounding society, monasticism sprang up to preserve the purity of faith.

Hilda, an Anglo-Saxon abbess, shows the place that could be held by women in the seventh century. A person of commanding appearance, wearing the flowing white robes and dark headdress of Christians in Bible times, for more than twenty years she was administrator, teacher and spiritual guide of the double monastery at Whitby, where men and women worked and prayed together. Hilda had been brought up by Queen Ethelberga, whose father founded the See of Canterbury and whose mother established the first place of Christian worship there.[19] Bishop Aidan of Iona asked Hilda's help, and in response she opened her first monastery. Her educational work included the training of the poet Caedmon and five English bishops (one of whom baptized Bede). While abbess, she presided over an important synod at Whitby in which the Roman dating of Easter was accepted with far-reaching effects. She died in 680 while urging her people to preserve harmony in the church.

As time went on, women participated in missionary work and in reform movements affecting the development of Christian institutions. Catherine of Siena, a Dominican tertiary who lived in the fourteenth century, heard God's call to both active service and contemplation. When the Black Death swept Europe, she did nursing, but she is chiefly known for her efforts to restore unity to the church. The period is remembered in church history for the location of the papacy at Avignon just prior to the struggle of rival popes for office. A woman of fine intelligence and disciplined prayer, Catherine was influential with two popes, Gregory XI and Urban VI. Late one night, a story goes, when she was guest in the palace of a noblewoman at Genoa, Pope Gregory appeared at the door, dressed in the plain black cassock of a priest. Without identifying himself to the night watchman, he sent Catherine what appeared to be a priest's message, "My need is great. Admit me, in the name of Jesus Christ."

"Bring him to me at once," Catherine replied.[20] The pope had come to unburden his anxious concern to this woman who lived close to God and had insight into church problems. Gregory said that he left Catherine's presence "strengthened and edified."

Urban VI summoned her to Rome, before return to the Vatican itself became possible, and asked her to speak to the assembled cardinals on the schism that was tearing the church apart. Her words moved him as they had moved his predecessor. When she had finished, Urban said, "Behold

my brethren, how contemptible we are before God, when
we give way to fear. This poor woman puts us to shame,
whom I call so, not out of contempt, but by reason of the
weakness of her sex, which should make her timid even if
we were confident. It is she who now encourages us." [21]
There is a difference between masculine and feminine
strength which makes mutual ministry indispensable in mo-
ments of crisis.

Protestants sometimes think their leaders had a monopoly
on efforts to renew the church during the Reformation period, and that Catholic reform came later as a kind of defense measure. The truth is that many Catholics were
laboring at the same time for many of the same ends. Teresa of Avila, a contemporary of Martin Luther, struggled
to renew the Carmelite Order to which she belonged. She
led an active as well as contemplative life, facing controversy with powerful anti-reform forces in the church, but
won papal recognition for her reformed (Discalced) Carmelite Order. Along with her organizational ability she exercised a marvelous gift of teaching through her writings
on prayer, which are still studied. An article, "Doctor of
the Church," in *The New Catholic Encyclopedia* declares:
"No woman has been proclaimed [Doctor], although St.
Teresa of Avila has popularly been given the title because
of the influence of her spiritual teaching; it would seem
that no woman is likely to be named because of the link between this title and the teaching office, which is limited to
males." [22] Is it presumptuous to ask if that office should not
be re-examined? What is the relation of the gift of teaching, bestowed by the Holy Spirit, to the office? Does teaching occur when people learn or when authority speaks? If
the office precedes rather than follows the gift, and communication does not occur, though good will is present, what
does this cost the church?

Monasticism, which had changed considerably since its
inception, was rejected by Protestants during the Reformation. Henceforth the home was to be woman's place, mar-

riage and motherhood her career. While the Roman Catholic Church had recognized marriage as a sacrament,[23] its emphasis on virginity as the higher form of Christian commitment caused many of both sexes to feel that God's call to them made single life preferable. (In this they were following Paul's advice,[24] which modern scholars believe grew out of his expectation of the imminent return of Christ.) Protestant reformers, however, believed that marriage is compatible with the highest call and rejected virginity as an aid to the service of God.

But even with the tenor of the times militating against work outside their homes, Protestant women felt summoned to public ministry without being initially aware of what was happening. Anne Hutchinson, daughter of an Anglican clergyman, left England with her husband for the New World in 1934. The King James Version of the Bible had been in circulation less than a quarter of a century and Anne was an avid student of it. Several of her women friends in New England asked her to help them understand it and a small study group began in her home. The gathering was so stimulating that attendance grew; ministers became uneasy about this congregating of females and took Anne to task. She pointed out Titus 2:3–5, where older women are exhorted to teach their younger sisters, but any response from her sex, save humble obedience to the clerical word, was intolerable: Anne faced real trouble. One cannot judge the motives of contemporaries, let alone those of people who lived in the seventeenth century. Probably they felt justified in defending the pure Gospel teaching, as they understood it, but it was also hard to watch women, not to mention men, drinking in a female preacher's words with more relish than they exhibited for their carefully prepared scholarly sermons. In any case, when no approach, buttered or unbuttered, silenced the woman, they excommunicated her and drove the family out of Massachusetts.[25] Even this did not give them rest, for they were overtaken by the uneasy feeling that she might damage her new neighbors; accordingly, they sent a delegation to demand of her husband, who was now a magistrate in Rhode Island, that he put a stop to her talk. He bluntly refused, saying, "I think her to be a dear saint and servant of God." [26] He must have known; they were the parents of fifteen children. After his death, however, Mrs. Hutchinson, with the youngest members of her family, took a homesite near the present Pelham, New York, where white men incited Indians to put them to death.

Desiring freedom for themselves, the colonists were often reluctant to grant it to others. The Hutchinsons believed in the inner guidance of grace, a view which found strong support among Friends and Baptists. Both the city of Boston and the church of which Anne had been a member honored her as an exponent of civil and religious freedom more than 250 years after her death. But even while she lived, she did not stand alone. Quaker women were being summoned to "come up into God's service;" indeed they were sometimes even put to death, along with men, for their faith.

The Holy Spirit spoke also to women in other churches, giving Catherine Booth the strange intimation, "I will make thee a mother of nations." A bright, adventurous girl, she had married a young English Methodist preacher in 1855; both were ardently religious but Catherine had no idea of being anything except a good wife and mother. When her husband, William, became an evangelist she knew the sacrifice this entailed, but shared his growing sense of mission. She had already had three children and was expecting her fourth when the visit of an American woman evangelist started an uproar in England over "female ministry." Uninvolved in the controversy herself, Catherine wrote in defense of the woman. Then, several months after the birth of her baby, while she was seated in chapel listening to her husband, the experience that changed everything took place:

I felt the Holy Spirit come to me . . . It seemed as if a voice said to me, "Now if you were to go and testify, you know I would bless it to your own soul, as well as to the people . . ." I almost jumped up, and said, "No, Lord, it is the old thing over again. But I cannot do it!" I felt as though I would sooner die than speak. And then the Devil said, "Besides, you are not prepared. You will look like a fool, and will have nothing to say." He made a mistake. He overreached himself for once. It was this word that settled it. "Ah," I said, "this is just the point. I have never been willing to be a fool for Christ. Now I will be one!" Without stopping another moment I rose up from my seat and walked down the aisle.[27]

The fervor of her address soon brought many invitations to preach. Sometimes her congregations numbered into the thousands with more men present than women. During one series of meetings, she preached twelve consecutive Sundays for one hour from one text, "Go, work today in my vineyard." Her husband became father of the Salvation Army and she became its mother. Their eight children spread all over the world, with most of them following in their parents' footsteps. Their daughter Evangeline was General of the world-wide Salvation Army from 1934 to 1939 when she retired at the age of seventy-four.

In all these examples, women were called to teach, preach, organize and direct the work of the church all over the world, not displacing men but standing beside them. They did this without any ordination save that of God; but another day was coming.

WHO STARTED ORDAINING WOMEN?

Less than a hundred years ago, seminaries were still closed to women. It was only in 1834 that Oberlin Collegiate Institute (now Oberlin College) became the first coeducational, privately controlled nondenominational school in the United States. Oberlin prided itself on its liberality; a center for antislavery activities, it operated an underground railroad. Students once rescued a black man from law officers who intended to send him back "where he belonged." They were jailed for disturbing the peace and the incident got nation-wide attention. But Oberlin had no idea to what lengths its liberality would be stretched where women were concerned.

Antoinette Brown, after finishing her college work there, horrified her alma mater by applying for entrance to the seminary. Meeting after meeting was held to devise ways of keeping her out but the charter stated that all privileges open to men were also open to women. (The assumption had been that women would not want anything but a short literary course. But seminary!) Finally, Professor Morgan of the Department of Biblical Literature was delegated to tell her that they would have kept her out if they could, but since that was impossible, they would do their very best to teach her. The Ladies' Board, composed mostly of professors' wives, did not give up so easily. A rule was made restricting graduate students from teaching undergraduates in an effort to limit means of self-support for women. Antoinette's parents disapprovingly withdrew their assistance. She was refused a license to preach. Other help came, however, and she graduated in 1850, but the seminary would not list her with the men. Years later, however, she was listed with her class; in 1878 she was awarded an honorary Master's degree, and in 1908 was made a Doctor of Divinity.[28]

Antoinette preached her first sermon in Henrietta, New York, her home town, and, in 1853, was ordained to the ministry of the Congregational Church. Horace Greeley and Charles A. Dana, editors of the *New York Tribune* and the *New York Sun,* were so impressed with lectures they had heard her give prior to her ordination that they called public attention to the fact that she was not permitted to speak when she attended the World's Temperance Convention in New York City as a delegate in 1853. Greeley wrote:

> This convention has completed three of its four business sessions, and the results may be summed up as follows: First Day—Crowding a woman off the platform. Second Day—Gagging her. Third Day—Voting that she shall stay gagged. Having thus disposed of the main question, we presume the incidentals will be finished this morning.[29]

They offered to provide a hall in New York City and a salary of one thousand dollars a year with board if she would agree to preach there regularly. She considered herself too inexperienced for such work and went instead to South Butler, New York, where she served the Congregational Church for three hundred dollars a year.

Two years after her ordination, she married Samuel Blackwell, a prosperous hardware merchant who, in sympathy with her career, made it possible for her to continue professional work while rearing six children, writing ten books and leading various reform movements.[30]

The situation Antoinette Brown faced was only a little less acute for some of the oldest women who responded to my questionnaire. One in her eighties relates that her great-aunt had received the degree of Doctor of Medicine in 1851. When, as a child of ten, my respondent visited this relative, a woman minister was a guest at dinner. The adults talked about how much more difficult it was for a woman to go into the ministry than into medicine but the child found the guest so charming that she resolved then and there to be a minister herself. Later, someone told her she would have to study Greek to follow that profession, so she took three years of it in high school.

She taught for a while after graduating from college but when she proposed entering seminary her mother was against it. "Try out the work of the church first," she advised. The great-aunt's woman minister friend was no longer living but had been survived by her husband, also a minister, who took the girl to a congregation from which a woman minister was retiring. "I was a member of the Presbyterian Church," my respondent says, "and my pastor wished to bring the matter before the Presbytery." In 1912, an overture was sent to the General Assembly, the Presbytery asking permission to take me under its care as a student for the ministry. The General Assembly said "NO," but she, too, received her divinity degree from Oberlin in 1917.

A number of similar experiences are related by older women. One explained that the president of her seminary did not approve of women going into the ministry and wanted her to prepare instead to teach Bible in college. A young professor encouraged her and she was permitted to take the same courses the men took but could not be graduated from the theological department with them. She has been a successful pastor for many years.

Hartford Theological Seminary in Connecticut was the first to open its doors willingly to female students. This was in 1889. The faculty, conscious of new opportunities for women, felt they must be fitted to respond both scholastically and practically. While they were received "on precisely the same terms as men," this did not mean that their ordination to the ministry of the church was contemplated. Rather, missionary work at home and abroad, Christian teaching and organized charitable work were seen as suitable fields for their endeavor.[31] In 1918, the seminary faculty took the position that it did not train women for the ministry because of the attitude of the churches which did not ask them to do so. Two years later, however, two professors formulated a new policy that was adopted by the faculty: "In view of the changed attitude of the churches toward the ordination of women, we no longer require women to state on entering the seminary that they do not expect to enter the ministry." [32] Up to this time, only two women a year had been received into the degree program for Bachelor of Divinity. No seminary money was put into scholarships for them but the Women's Board provided two for each class. This limitation was trusted to prevent over-population of the institution by the fair sex.

The Methodist Church, because of its polity, faced a more difficult situation than Free Churches when women asked for ordination in the early twentieth century. They were granted local preachers' licenses in 1919 and provision was made for their ordination in 1924. In 1919, the American Association of Women Ministers came into being through the initiative of M. Madeline Southard (see Appendix 3). The Methodist Church, however, could not take the chance of giving women the same status as men because of popular resistance to their role as ministers, so there was no assurance of placement for them until 1956, when they were permitted to become members of Annual Conferences with the same security as men. Prior to 1956, ten of my respondents left the Methodist Church because they felt they could serve more effectively with full status elsewhere.[33] As one former Methodist respondent stated, "I had no desire to fight the Woman's Suffrage Movement all over again." Like twenty-six other respondents, she entered the Congregational ministry and now holds a conference post.

Also in 1956, the United Presbyterian Church U.S.A. began ordaining women; previously, they had been only permitted to become ruling elders. Eight of my respondents left the Presbyterian Church prior to 1956 in search of wider opportunity for ministry. Several years later, the Presbyterian Church U.S. (southern) began ordaining women.

EVALUATING THE EXPERIENCE

For churches to feel secure in ordaining women, they would like to have some idea of how the plan will work, but how can they know unless women are first ordained? One way is to study the experience of churches that have been free enough to try.

Dr. Thomas A. Tripp, Director of town and country work for the Congregational Christian Board of Home Missions, made a survey, in 1948, of the women ministers of that denomination. He found that "women compare favorably with men in effectiveness in the ministry in similar types of parishes. In rural churches women excel when compared with men. Notwithstanding the fact that Congregational Christian rural churches served by women average smaller than the norm for all rural churches of the Fellowship, the performance of those served by women runs consistently higher that that of the total. In comparison to the number of members per church, parishes served by women are doing better than usual work in every point recorded in the *Yearbook* annual reports." [34] As a result of his study, Dr. Tripp felt that women should be encouraged to prepare for and seek ordination. Feeling that at least one thousand women could be absorbed into the ministry of his church over a period of ten years, he recommended that churches be encouraged to accept them as pastors and that associations receive them as persons meeting the requirements of acceptable ministerial standards. [35]

Women working for seminary degrees are sometimes urged to write theses on the place of women in the church. Research done by Mary H. Candy revealed that, after the first few years of adjustment in churches previously served by men, the appreciation of women as pastors rose sharply. They were praised for their efforts in improving the church plant, their organizational and business talents, ability to get people to work together, their care for the sick, knowledge of Christian education and understanding of the emotional problems of the young. Mrs. Candy's sample was small: fifty questionnaires were sent out to both men and women, with thirty-six replies received; geographic distribution was wide, however, and four denominations were represented. Interestingly enough, in evaluating pastoral service, seven said men and women were equally effective; twenty-five said women were more effective; four said men were more effective. The significant fact is that, after churches had been served by women for ten years or more, little difference between men and women was noted; the women were ministers, not ladies trying to fill the shoes of men.[36]

There is one positive sociological factor present in the appreciation of women as pastors which should not be overlooked. Just as society expects that men should be administrators, it feels that women are natural counselors. Probably this begins with the typical exchange of early childhood: "Daddy, I want to . . ." "Well, go and ask your mother." The heavy demands upon men as breadwinners, with success often involving considerable travel and taking work home even on weekends, have resulted in women taking a preponderant part in guiding children and youth. When one also realizes how much of the counseling work of the church is with children, youth and women, it can readily be seen that female clergy have a certain advantage. Male pastors may be excellent counselors, as a number of respondents point out, but it always seems more natural to turn to a woman in pain or distress. One respondent says that just as a man may be too paternalistic or dictatorial in his pastoral work, a woman must be careful not to become too motherly or over-protective. The faults as well as the strengths associated with family roles can be carried over into church work.

Since our society sees men as administrators, women are supposed to be deficient in this role. How do female pastors cope with this problem? A number prefer not to cope with it at all and have chosen to serve on multiple staffs as associates, assistants or ministers of education, positions that do not place the full burden of church management on them. The majority of women, probably due to both their own temperamental bent and the influence of upbringing, do not find administrative work the most enjoyable part of their task. But this does not mean that women ministers have been poor administrators. Most of them know that they cannot neglect organization. Being conscientious, they find out what is necessary—few men or women have learned administration in the seminary. When women are serving as pastors, there are few complaints over what they are able to do about organization. By the time they are out in the field they have faced the hard fact that "a woman has to be twice as good to get half as far."

Besides, a minority of women thoroughly enjoy administrative work and have special gifts in this area. Elsie Johns, for example, a Methodist pastor in Michigan, was asked by her bishop to go and see if she could revive a dying church. She found a building with every window broken and no heating plant; on the pulpit a note had been left: "There are no members and no money. Here's the key." A school official told her, "Go back where you came. Even by police statistics it is a frightful area." She made calls from door to door, but for four Sundays faced an empty church. Then two women came, bringing their children, and she started a Sunday School. At the end of fourteen years, she was able to give up secular employment; the church could support her. Today, more than twenty-five years later, she serves the same church with a membership well over a thousand. Along with her love of people, Miss Johns has evidently learned how to administer a parish effectively. She has worked with her district superintendents and bishops, studying the material prepared by her denomination on such subjects as stewardship methods, Christian education and service to the community and to mankind. Her church is living proof that young people want to participate when they see authentic belief in action.

Women themselves often weigh the advisability of seeking ordination. In listing the various forms of ministry pursued by respondents (see Preface), it was significant that there were eighteen ministers of Christian Education as against three directors. A generation ago, women who prepared to become directors of education had no thought of ordination. They sought a degree in their own field and did not pursue divinity studies, simply taking a few seminary courses as electives. But from one correspondent after another I have learned that, while a considerable number of women still wish to specialize in Christian Education, they also wish to take a full seminary course, to receive ordination, and to share the ministry with men on a basis of equality. The reasons my respondents give for this are worth considering.

1. The inferior status of the director, based on her shorter period of study, had made education a step-child of the church. One assistant pastor with this responsibility says that ordination has been a real assistance in raising the level of educational work in the congregation because people now see it as an aspect of the total ministry of the church rather than as a little department by itself.

2. The church's teaching ministry must be considered part of the ministry of the word. If not, what is it? There should be no dichotomy between the ministry of teaching and the pulpit ministry, including the sacraments. A seminary senior explained how several of her professors had helped her to make up her mind to seek ordination. "They suggested that if I was ordained, it would be natural to turn to me in training sessions, etc. to lead in worship or perhaps to lead communion. It was also pointed out that a more

meaningful experience can be had at a camp or at a training session for teachers if the person doing the training can also be the worship leader and doesn't need to call in someone else."

3. Those who feel drawn to a *ministry* of education increasingly recognize their need for a solid theological basis in their specialization. A young woman in an Eastern city speaks for a growing number: "I enjoy the tasks of preaching, counseling and calling and do not see my job description in Christian Education as prohibiting these activities. I do not feel that people throw up a barrier against me when I preach just because I am a woman." These respondents do not expect to preach every Sunday but they want to be known for what they are—ministers.

4. The old idea that men were ministers, women directors, has resulted in a paucity of male leadership in the educational work of the church, where it is greatly needed. Most respondents favor teamwork between men and women, rather than stereotyping ministries on the basis of sex. Rigid roles have caused an appalling loss to the church. Should not persons be allowed to develop their personal gifts and thus to find their true mission in the world?

WILL OTHER CHURCHES ORDAIN WOMEN?

As women find more places of leadership in modern society, pressure is put upon churches having only male ministers to change their ways or to justify them by adequate reasons. The latter becomes more difficult as time goes on.

Woman's work in the Church of England has been under consideration for the last hundred years.[37] The participation of the Episcopal Church in the United States in the Consultation on Church Union with bodies which do ordain women makes the question seem urgent. The dilemma for the whole Anglican communion is well posed in a recently completed study, *Women in Ministry*, the Report of the Working Party set up jointly by the Ministry Committee of the Advisory Council for the Church's Ministry and the Council for Women's Ministry in the Church. The Working Party could not reach a consensus. Some members saw no conclusive objection to the ordination of women, but neither were they prepared to say unequivocally that there were in fact no such objections and that the time for such a step had arrived. Others considered ordination for women to be both right and opportune. "All are agreed that until the Church resolves this matter, it will be almost impossible to make any clear definition of women's part in ministry. It should be noted that if the priesthood were to be open to women, so in principle would be the episcopate." [38]

While this problem may, on the surface, seem academic, it can change the lives of individual women. The intention of the late Bishop James Pike to ordain Mrs. Phyllis Edwards to the position of "perpetual deacon" was given national publicity when it was blocked.[39] What is not so well known, however, is that Mrs. Edwards' case is not isolated. One respondent, Phyllis Ingram, a trim, attractive young widow, sent the following letter individually to every active bishop (and some retired) in her church.

This letter constitutes an appeal to the House of Bishops as the only body competent to deal with my situation. The dilemma I face is faced by others at the present time, and will confront many more in the future.

I have the qualifications and training for the ordained ministry. Last May I graduated from the Virginia Theological Seminary with a B. D., cum laude having completed the regular course including clinical pastoral training and two years of field work in a parish. My vocation has been tested and its validity, I think, established.

The seminary recommended me for ordination, and the

parish in which I have worked would have called me as an assistant; but since I am a woman this Church is unable to recognize me. Lacking that recognition, I cannot be called to minister where I am otherwise qualified to do so, in a parish where the demand for the ministry of the sacraments is too great for the priest to meet. I am in effect dismissed from consideration not as a person, nor yet as a person lacking qualifications, but solely because of my sex.

Not being in Holy Orders will inhibit my ministry else-where as in the parish to which I refer; but I do not wish to have to seek ordination in another body. May I appeal to you, therefore, to accord to me and to others the right to have the call to ministry judged and recognized on the basis of qualifications and training alone, as surely it ought to be.

The replies of the bishops reveal how far the Episcopal Church is from a solution to this problem. A retired bishop wrote her, "Your training fits you wonderfully for a lay position. I cannot believe your parish or seminary gave any reason to believe the Church Canons would be changed. The position has been a clear one and you have no right to blame the Church if you followed your own will . . . You have been ill advised . . . Give your mind and heart to serve the Church as she makes it possible and not try to make conditions." An active bishop wrote, "I am sorry but I can't agree with you about women in Holy Orders; that is the Orders which men have been holding. This has noth-ing to do with integrity, training or call or anything else." Another, "I do not believe that the House of Bishops would entertain an appeal in a single case to Holy Orders in the Church."

Others, however, took a favorable attitude. One said, "Whether or not the place of women in the Church is scheduled to come up, I do not know, but I hope it will, and that some progress will be made to do away with the stigma of sex." Another sent a long, handwritten reply,

"Your letter to the bishops of the Episcopal Church which was received prior to our recent meeting touched me deeply. I can find no theological reason against the ordination of women to the sacred ministry, and no practical reason that would not be equally valid for arguing against their admission to the fields of law, medicine and a score of other professions in which they have proved themselves as competent as men. There remains only prejudice—as strong apparently and unfortunately among the women of the laity as among the men. If as is [staying in the laity] is insufficient, if your vocation leads you beyond, I should understand your making application to a branch of the Church which currently accepts women for the sacred ministry, for I have no doubts as to the validity of such a ministry or of the denominations in which it may be exercised."

The faculty of Mrs. Ingram's seminary went on record in the fall of 1966 as favoring the ordination of women, a shift from the position held at the time of her entrance as a student.

Mrs. Ingram felt pushed to a choice between obedience to Christ and remaining in the Episcopal Church. She is now an ordained minister of the United Church of Christ, serving as assistant pastor in a large city parish. Three other ordained respondents have left the Episcopal Church.

Mrs. Ingram makes the interesting observation that the tenor of the replies she received did not show a cleavage between those oriented toward Protestantism as favoring her position and Anglo-Catholics as opposing. Her conclusion here is borne out by other (non-Episcopal) respondents. One was told by an Anglo-Catholic priest, "I believe that you are more truly called by God into the ministry of the Church than some of my colleagues." Another mentions that Roman Catholic priests have given her the greatest encouragement she has ever received in the ministry. A third has been invited to speak from the pulpit of a Roman Catholic Church.

A second point made by Mrs. Ingram is that clergy of her former church seem blind to clerical prejudice, laying it at the door of the laity. Without doubt there is lay prejudice, but I have long felt that Episcopal laity are bearing more than their fair share of responsibility in this matter. Twice, when I was serving a church, Episcopal laymen accepted my professional services when a clergyman of their own communion was inaccessible. In one case at least, it would have been quite easy to secure a male clergyman of another denomination. I have also been told by a member of the Episcopal Church that clergy express fear of a woman bishop when lay persons seem disposed to vote for the ordination of women to the priesthood. While these are only straws in the wind, they do lend some slight support to Mrs. Ingram's conclusion.

It is rarely easy for a woman to leave her church. It is the fellowship of persons through whose witness she has, at least in part, learned about God. Her dearest friends are there. She is familiar with its forms of worship, with its vocabulary, with its way of working. In a very real sense that church has brought her to the place where she can inwardly hear the divine voice and where she can know herself as a responsible person and act with decision. The women who have left churches which could not ordain them to the kind of ministry they were impelled to give have done so with a heavy heart.

The Lutheran Churches of the United States have also been facing the question of the ordination of women. The Division of Theological Studies of the Lutheran Council in the United States of America, because of divergent views that have been emerging within American Lutheranism, has been asked by the churches to look for a common Lutheran position on this matter. The Missouri Synod group, in the past, has taken a strong stand against women exercising pastoral office. The Report of the Commission on Theology and Church Relations, in its document, *Woman Suf-*

frage in the Church, reveals that considerable progress has been made by that denomination in the past decade and that biblical studies are undergirding all the work. Adhering closely to Pauline and other biblical texts, the study brings out the fact that it is not so much delegated authority to which the apostle objected as a domineering attitude on woman's part, a "usurping of authority." Other Lutheran groups in the United States, while not ordaining women, have made no doctrinal pronouncements on the subject. Theological conferences are planned which will consider the ordination of women in the broader context of church, ministry and ministry of the laity.[40]

During the Second Vatican Council the Roman Catholic Church received a resolution from an organization of its own churchwomen, St. Joan's International Alliance. This group, which originated as a Catholic Woman's Suffrage Society, passed the following resolution at its annual meeting in 1964: "St. Joan's International Alliance reaffirms its loyalty and filial devotion, and expresses its conviction that should the Church in her wisdom and in her good time decide to extend to women the dignity of the priesthood, women would be willing and eager to respond." [41]

Mrs. Catherine McCarthy, Auditor at the Second Vatican Council and former President of the National Council of Catholic Women, reports that sixteen interventions were made on behalf of the recognition of women. Leo Cardinal Suenens said, at the third session, "The Church must abandon the masculine superiority complex which ignores the spiritual power of women . . . We must learn to respect woman in her true dignity and to appreciate her part in the plan of God." [42] The late Archbishop Hallinan of Atlanta, Georgia, made a written intervention at the last session of the Council. After recognizing the complementary role of woman as an equal partner of man, the Archbishop asked whether the church has given the leadership that Christ by word and example clearly showed he expected of her. "In proclaiming the equality of men and women, the Church must act as well as speak by fraternal testimony, not only in abstract doctrine." [43] The logic of his position led him to call for the ordination of women. [44] Some priests in the Netherlands are also taking a favorable position. [45] Two doctoral dissertations have reached conclusions supporting the ordination of women: one by Jose Idigoras in Lima, Peru, the other by Haye van der Meer working with Karl Rahner. [46] Hans Küng told Mrs. Elizabeth Bussing, Secretary of the Committee to Study the Proper Place of Women in the Church's Ministry (Episcopal), in a telephone interview, "There are two factors to consider regarding the ordination of women. The first is that there are no dogmatic or biblical reasons against it. The second is that there are psychological and sociological factors to be considered. The solution to the problem depends on the sociological conditions of the time and place. It is entirely a matter of cultural circumstances." [47] Despite these favorable indications, there is no doubt that opposition within the Roman Catholic Church will be strong if and when such a possibility becomes more serious.

The Orthodox Churches are perhaps least ready to open their ministry to women. The direction of development in churches, as in individuals, depends to a large extent upon their geographic location, their experience, and internal pressures of one kind and another. The Eastern Churches have lived close to Islam where women are repressed more than in Christian lands. While women in Western Churches have been active in missionary enterprises, Orthodoxy has had to fight for its very life; such a beleaguered psychology does not provide opportunities where women might have been able to work along with men. Orthodox women have raised no sustained protest to their status. In addition, since it is difficult to distinguish the dynamism of spiritual witness in the Bible from its historical frame of reference, we should bear in mind that Orthodox theology works from a biblical anthropology derived from the second creation story (Genesis 2). How is this related to the first creation story (Genesis 1) and to the revelation of God in Christ? [48] Much ecumenical sharing will be necessary before biblical and theological interpretations stand any chance of reconciliation.

A part of the answer may come as men and women together consider the call some women believe they have received to the church's ministry of word and sacrament and as together they study the actual work done by those women who are already ordained. It is to this call and work that we now turn.

2.

A Sense of Mission

The church still speaks of God's call to the ministry but it is not as easy to say what is meant by this as it once was. Are we referring to an invasion of consciousness by some mysterious internal voice? This could as easily be an indication of mental illness as of divine invitation. Could the divine call be the sudden awareness of an impression previously received subliminally through reading or social contact? The behavioral sciences have made us aware of hitherto unsuspected possibilities of self-deception and projection upon divinity of unknown but entirely human mental functions. Today we prefer to proceed with caution in a field where so little is known and so much is surmised.

But having said that, it must be added that the behavioral sciences, quite as much as religion, bring certain preconceived modes of interpretation to experience. It is as unscientific to assume that there is no God who calls anyone to do anything as it is to make confident statements about his word and action. Neither *a priori* assertions nor religious faith should be confused with verified hypotheses. What is important for this book, however, is the fact that although few women ministers are naive about the complexity of motivation, the majority still speak of being called by God to the work they are trying to do.

CALLED IN CHILDHOOD

A child growing up in a Christian community which invites free and happy participation may little by little identify himself with the church's mission. After all, it is easy to pick up attitudes and values of admired adults if one has not been subjected to moralistic pressures and over-direction. The action of the Holy Spirit in motivating men and women can resemble either a gentle breeze or a gale. "As I see it now, my call to the ministry was implicit in my coming to know God when I was eleven," says Gretchen Hall, United Church of Christ minister in Connecticut. "At any rate through my high school years I haunted the church so much that when I came home from any event I was greeted, 'Well, did you lock the church tonight?' It was a beautiful building to haunt and the people I met there were excellent folks for a teen-ager to idealize." Many respondents refer to the influence of one or both parents, pastors, teachers or older friends. "I wanted to become a teacher like Jesus from the time I was in second grade," reports one woman who teaches in public school and is minister of a church that would be closed except for her part-time service.

It never occurred to her that the ordained ministry was not a suitable profession for her sex. Don't girls growing up go to Sunday School, where they participate equally with boys? At youth camps and conferences they hear lectures, take courses, join in discussions, and are challenged to

Christian commitment and vocation. There is no suggestion that a response regarding the ministry is expected from boys only; many women trace their first intimation of a life work to such summer events.

A call in childhood, however, is not always like this; it may come through intense, almost explosive, agony. Mary Murray had a ten-year-old sister who was her shadow. Suddenly the little girl was burned beyond hope of recovery, and Mary sat on the edge of their bed for several days listening to her sister tell her she could hear angels singing, "They are coming closer and closer." She wanted Mary to hear them, too, and to go along to meet them. After the child's death, Mary found the emptiness of her room intolerable. Night after night she cried herself to sleep, and yet, during this period, she felt that God was very near to her; she talked with him: "I promised the Lord that if he would guide me and show me what he wanted me to do with my life, I'd do it, cost what it might, and that I'd like to live my life not only for him but for my little sister, too."

Mary had to work her own way through school. Then, when a lonely, hard mission post among the Crow Indians in Montana opened up, she felt that this was the work she wanted to do. While there, she preached, taught, served Communion, conducted funeral services and performed marriages, without being ordained. Under Montana law, missionaries had the right to perform marriages. The nearest clergyman was a hundred miles away over gumbo roads; without missionary leadership, many Indians would have made common-law alliances.

Mary was so small and alone that a boy worried about her. "Why don't you get married?" he asked.

"I haven't had time," she laughed.

"Well, you should take a day off and do it."

When the Second World War broke out, her board asked her to go to Detroit to work among the thousands of "trailerites" employed in defense plants there. She lived in a trailer among them. "They didn't want to go to the big city churches so I felt that I must take the church to them. I asked for a 'church on wheels' and a big trailer was fixed up that I could haul around to the seventeen parks on the outskirts of the city." When attendance outgrew the Trailer Chapel, the people built a church with cement blocks donated by Catholic businessmen. Although pastor there, Mary also worked in the other parks. Since Michigan law required ordination for the solemnizing of marriages, she finally sought and obtained this status.

Asked whether the rigors of such a life were not too much for women, Miss Murray insisted, "God gives us strength for the things he calls us to do. In any case, physical strength is not the only kind." After twenty-one years of this ministry, she took that day off to get married and is now pastor of three Baptist Churches in Wisconsin.

CALLED TO BE ONESELF

In their effort to describe experience in current terminology, some respondents discuss their attraction to the ministry as the discovery or development of personal identity. The case of Marilynn Rushton, a minister's wife, is illustrative. When Marilynn arrived in Milwaukee to begin work as associate pastor of a United Methodist Church, she was interviewed by a reporter for *The Milwaukee Journal* who headlined his story, "Mini-skirted Minister Eager to Know Her Kenwood Flock." The *Journal* representative was not the only one who, by looking for a type, failed to discover a person. A church member inquired, "Do you think it quite appropriate, my dear, for a minister to wear a dress as short as this?" But Mrs. Rushton, an attractive brunette in her twenties, sees no reason why a woman minister should make herself conspicuously different from other young women. "I feel that as long as I can be myself, part of which means being a woman, I will be accepted as myself. It is important for people to know me as a person rather than a type." When she is honestly herself, she is convinced, it is easier for others to be themselves with her.

A graduate of Drew Theological Seminary, Mrs. Rushton's preparation for the ministry had been more than academic. She was director of education in a bilingual, interracial storefront church in Jersey City, New Jersey, an experience which opened her eyes to the racist sickness of the institutional church. "I was ashamed of my white skin because I realized I was part of a community that had been against Negroes." She also worked with the migrant ministry in New York during the summer and did in-service clinical training at a mental hospital as well as being pastor of a rural church.

Why, however, does she stay in the church if she feels it is "sick"? She stays because she believes it is the vehicle with the greatest potential for relating the Gospel of Christ to the world, offering her the best opportunity to serve others and to be an instrument of change in society. "The church provides a framework for meeting people in depth. You go into their homes and schools, share their happiness in marital counseling and at weddings, visit them in hospitals, stand beside them in their grief at funerals; in all of this, the Gospel must be preached and the work of the church be administered. I believe that the Christ who is universal and everywhere must be enabled to take root in the world through human lives; the life of our broken world must be encountered and transformed."

If anyone wonders how she expects to do all this as a married woman, she has an answer for that, too: "The fact that I am married is a sign to others that I have accepted my role and rejoice in being a woman and a wife. My being in the ministry seems to enrich our marriage and is a real part of how my husband and I are together. It will be the same when we have children and share our life with them."

The style of marriage is definitely changing and young women are finding it possible to do things that would not have been feasible even ten or fifteen years ago. While many young women in urban settings are developing a pattern of daily work similar to Marilynn Rushton's, until quite recently the expectations of one's spouse and social group often interfered with personal happiness.

The changed attitude toward women, however, has been finding expression in liberal circles for some time. Joyce Smith, Unitarian-Universalist pastor and mother of three teen-agers, did not enter the ministry until her children were well along in school. She has been blessed with an understanding husband, a professor of economics. "When I wanted to become pastor of a church after finishing seminary," she explained, "he moved with me. Earlier, while he was developing his career, I went wherever he wanted and was as supportive as possible as a homemaker and mother. Later, he returned the support in full measure because he realized this was very important to me and because he found his own work so satisfying. He was able to get a position in almost any area I would be able to go, making my placement much easier. In the future we will consider the needs of both careers before we make a move." Her husband is a member of the church she serves and helps her unofficially wherever he can. At first her children had to adjust to her new role, but now seem to take pride in it. "They realize that it may prevent the possibility of over-dominating their lives, either today or later when they are on their own."

Mrs. Smith thinks a person belongs in the ministry only if "it is the only thing you could have done, the only person you could have become. A call is the sense of being who you are." It integrates one's intellectual, emotional and moral commitments into a community of concern for others.

If we turn the clock back a little farther, we find that few women attempted careers, as a usual thing, until children were already on their own. Even then, the common pattern was for a woman to give her time to volunteer work so that she was free to fit into all her husband's plans and interests. For example, a career in the ministry did not occur to Greta Snider until after the death of her husband, a professor in the Harvard Business School. Two of her children were married and two were practically through college. "I preferred to be occupied professionally rather than to be at home alone," she explains. "My husband and I had been active in bringing two small churches together; we had served in nearly every lay capacity. You know how much small churches depend on the leadership of interested laymen." Following his death, she entered Andover Newton Theological Seminary, served rural churches, took clinical training and, until recently, has been chaplain at Cambridge City and Mt. Auburn hospitals in Massachusetts. "I know a call to the ministry often means a definite hour and place," Mrs. Snider remarked, "when the urge to obey a specific summons becomes overwhelming. But my own experience has been a growing conviction that leisure time interests, friends and gifts were drawing me toward the ministry." Isn't this, too, an authentic call?

Martin Heidegger wrote, "We receive many gifts, of many kinds. But the highest and really most lasting gift given to us is always our essential nature, with which we are gifted in such a way that we are what we are only through it." [1] When entering the ministry seems the truest expression of what we are, is this not offering back to God in thanksgiving and for others the best gift he has given us?

CALLED BY THE WORLD'S NEED

By example and teaching, Jesus directed the attention of his followers to the world's need. Whenever the church and individual Christians have been at their best, they have been responsive to that need. Indeed, some of the worst crimes of history have been enacted when professed Christians forgot this. Claiming to have "sweetest fellowship with Jesus" while transporting a cargo of slaves, as more than one ship's captain is said to have done, has produced an evil for which generations of both white and black persons have not finished paying. Churches, too, can become so introverted that the main point of their existence is to preserve the status quo. Preoccupation with one's own soul and with institutional machinery has always been a mark of retrogression in the Christian religion.

"I saw a need" was a frequent response to the query, "Why did you go into the ministry?" Petite and feminine, Judith Coleman knew she had to be a minister "after a sort of Damascus Road experience in high school. Of course, I never dreamed of marrying a minister." But that is what happened, and her husband says, "What Judy decides to do with her life is as important as my own plans." [2] She is interested in working with people in forgotten places. While still in seminary, she took a year of clinical training in a neurological institute under the supervision of a psychiatrist. Many of the patients were retarded children; she had to learn how to relate to people as a basic part of this training.

Her next work was in a prison for women where half of the one hundred fifty inmates were under twenty-five years old and had been convicted of various offenses associated with the use of narcotics. At first, Mrs. Coleman found the women wary of "this young minister's thing," but she, along with a Roman Catholic colleague, slowly won them to participation. Instead of conducting Sunday worship by herself, she got them to do parts of the service. Discussions and role playing were a regular part of the Bible classes. "I tried to find out what questions they had," she explains, "then courses were planned to deal with subjects they proposed, such as racial prejudice, homosexuality, and the use of drugs." She stressed the need for recreational programs. "All we had was a sewing room and a laundry. A music director and an art teacher would have helped." She knows that this will require a long-term effort to arouse interest in both church and state.

One thing that distressed her was lack of communication between the church and the prison. This was overcome, to some extent, by getting twenty volunteers to visit on a friendly, non-counseling basis. (Her husband was student pastor of the local church.) Judith has now resigned her chaplaincy post in order to concentrate on getting a rehabilitation center or halfway house for women who have been in prison.

She and her husband believe the ministry of the future may lie in husband-wife teams where each can complement the work of the other. The problems they encounter are not so much with the laity as with clergy who do not see how a young wife can be "fulfilling her marriage vows" when she is so active outside her own home.

Several of the younger respondents to my questionnaire work in the inner city. Sometimes torn between the desire for a home of her own and "helping rootless, wandering, inadequate persons to find a home and self-value," one respondent thinks women may be able to make their best contribution through a specialized ministry rather than as "general practitioners." As in the medical and other professions, a need is seen for expertise in more phases of ministry than is possible in an assignment where assistance is called for in too many capacities. The importance of team ministries in ghetto areas is stressed. One widow believes that inner city work especially calls for leadership of both sexes: women heads of families can identify more easily with a woman, while children require a good male, as well as female, image for their mental and spiritual growth. In addition, a racially integrated ministry is needed to help overcome the temptation of minority groups to draw apart into isolated communities.

Young women sometimes seem ambivalent about the church as an institution in society. They are disappointed because it appears to be more concerned with its own life than with the surrounding world but many remain loyal because, deficient as it is, there is no other institution which has as its one goal "service to God through service to, for and with other persons." As one of them put it, "No work other than the ministry seemed meaningful enough to merit organizing my whole life around it."

My survey also drew responses from several women whose summer work in churches alerted them to the need for pastors in poverty-stricken areas of the South. They became acquainted with small, struggling churches that could not afford a man with a family, or where ministers' wives were reluctant to bring up children. Such churches were often intermittently served by men with little or no education, and whose spiritual understanding was open to question. A trained woman could find plenty to do.

The rural South has a religious vocabulary which is all but incomprehensible to sophisticated city-dwellers. One correspondent, just passing eighty, who has known that old South intimately, explains that she went there "because of an overwhelming desire to win souls for Christ and to minister to the needy, the sick and the unfortunate." She carried evangelistic fervor and sound education into a homesteading area which could appreciate the one and greatly needed the other. "In the early days, I worked in the backwoods sections, where I have assisted in making caskets for the dead and have been by the side of the doctors when the babies arrived." The denominational executive in that area told me she was a "solid citizen, a shepherdess of the flock whose capacity as a pastor to identify completely with her people has seldom been excelled. Churches which she served always grew." In 1965, her state conference (United Church of Christ) presented her with a Certificate of Honor in recognition of fifty-six years in the ministry. But if her denomination felt real retirement accompanied this honor, they were mistaken. "I shall be eighty my next birthday and still speak every Sunday morning—and I still sing solos—tho' I do not ask for too much of that sort of activity! Accidents have made it awkward for me to get about, but the folks seem not to mind, bless 'em." She still visits the "retired old folks," has some weddings and funerals, goes to the hospital when people are having major surgery, but no longer makes pastoral calls!

FINDING THE RIGHT LANE

Since the ministry is not regarded as a profession for women, many come to it by a long and winding road, even though they felt strongly attracted in that direction early in life. It took eighteen years for Dorothy Kling, an associate minister with special responsibility for education in a metropolitan area, to reach her goal. She was drawn to the work of the church in high school, but the depression kept her from going to college. She became secretarial assistant in the supervision of instruction in the Detroit public schools and in teacher training at Wayne University. A business office provided a good place to observe tensions between employers and employees; Dorothy recognized that Christian character on both sides helps to bridge the gap, and reflected on the church's concern in this area. Increasingly, "the materials going through my typewriter were no longer words going through a machine, but ideas which I was trying to incorporate into a philosophy of Christian education."

Feeling that her job offered small opportunity to put these new insights to work, over family protests, she gave more and more time to the church. When she finally fell ill, she realized she would have to make a choice between her job and a larger ministry: "Every time I said, 'No,' the question rose again. But if I said, 'Yes,' I still wasn't sure that was the answer. I decided I had to get off the fence and find out."

She faced eleven hours of formidable entrance examinations at the University of Chicago in order to enter the accelerated arts program. This hurdle was passed successfully; then she had to figure out how to support herself while carrying ten hours of graduate study during a leave of absence from the position she held in Detroit. When she visited the office of the field work director in search of church employment while going to school, he said, "You realize this has to be a tailor-made job, don't you?" It looked hopeless, but fifteen minutes after she left his office, she found a note at her hotel to call him. Right after interviewing her, he had discovered an unopened letter on his desk containing a request for a person to fill the "tailor-made job." "You're on your own. Sell yourself," he told her. Three months later she was director of Christian Education in a church.

She did not, however, jump to the conclusion that everything was settled. "It was only *after* I had been required to perform ministerial functions that I was able to affirm, 'This is it.' "

Miss Kling does not think a vivid sense of "being called" is the universal experience: "For many there are years of preparation, even blindness to God's will, but one ultimately discovers a unity of quest, interests, energies, talents, values, beliefs, and philosophy of life in the ministry if this is the work one should do."

When a girl says she wants to become a minister, the response from parents is seldom a smile and encouraging word. There are difficulties ahead for a woman with such a purpose, and those who love her do not want to see her hurt. Helen Lyman, a tall, willowy blonde United Church of Christ pastor in New Hampshire, was moved by a college course in New Testament to consider the ministry. Her family was opposed: "You can't do it. Who do you think you are—Maude Royden [pioneer woman minister in England]?" She dropped the idea and became a volunteer social worker. After that, she served as pastor's assistant for seven years. But the idea that the "basic and most urgent need of all sorts and conditions of men is spiritual" remained with her. She knew that was the need to which she wanted to give her best efforts.

During her seminary years, she was told by various conference ministers who came to interview students that there were few, if any, openings for women. Hearing of a woman minister who had also been a nurse, and who had found that preparation helpful, Miss Lyman entered nurses' training after seminary in the hope that "I might be accepted as a nurse if not as a minister. Inasmuch as I had long had a special interest in and concern for the rural church, I felt that a year of experience as a graduate nurse in rural public health would be valuable."

When she first tried to find a pastorate, Miss Lyman encountered several instances of strong prejudice against a woman minister. Some pulpit committees were not even willing to meet her. In her first parish, however, where she served thirteen years, although there apparently had been reservations about calling her, she felt accepted almost from the start. She was conscious, too, of how difficult it was for male clergy to accept a woman into what they considered a field suited only to men.

Miss Lyman is convinced that a woman can make a distinctive contribution in counseling. As a nurse, she was called in on almost every emergency that occurred in the community. "While I was called as a nurse, I was often able to act as a minister in cases of fatal accident, when sitting, sometimes for hours, with a dying patient." A pastor now, she feels the nursing experience has helped her work with doctors in the community, guiding her in relationships between patients and their families and bringing her into close contact with patients in both general and mental hospitals. Her neighbors say that she once saved a woodsman's life in a situation when a doctor could not be reached. What may look to us like lost time in reaching a profession is thus taken up into the purpose of God and used by him to make that vocation more productive.

Most high schools bypass the ministry completely when vocational possibilities are introduced to students. It is not surprising, then, that a man or woman may be well established in another occupation before the possibility of a church vocation even presents itself. This was the case with Emily Craig, who is now a United Church of Christ minister in North Madison, Connecticut. She had advanced ten years into a fascinating career with General Electric— doing lighting design layouts for individual residences, prominent national structures and high-rise apartment buildings—before receiving the first intimation that her real work was the ministry. During those years of professional advancement, the call to the ministry came to her in intermittent flashes as she saw how the church needed updating to meet the needs of children and young people. After a summer of concentration on how to invest her future, she decided to enter seminary where her training included opportunities to do field work with youth and adults. "When I changed occupations, I did not leave the profession of light behind," she told me, blue-gray eyes thoughtful, "but only changed to another form of illumination." She enjoys the administrative aspect of her pastoral work and looks forward to the day when she can plan the lighting of a church.

Gitta Morris, the staff reporter who interviewed Emily upon the latter's arrival in North Madison, started her news story, "The new minister at the Congregational Church fits well the preconceived idea of the perfect clergy—warm, wise, worldly and with a fine sense of humor. There is one incongruity, however. This minister . . . is a woman . . . It would seem that the ministry is just the profession that can benefit by a woman's touch and intuition." One detail that captivated the reporter was the ordination robe that Emily had made herself—"a magnificent shade of crimson, a unique and striking effect."

It is not uncommon for a woman to resist strenuously what she suspects might be a "call to the ministry." There are other ways to serve, she reasons, where less opposition would be encountered. Adele Spencer, a Presbyterian pastor in New York state, thought about these "other ways" while she was in college. After graduating, however, she worked with a small congregation of a different denomination long enough to feel that she might have a place in the ministry. Even in the seminary, self-doubt continued to plague her: "Maybe I'm not the right person for this kind of work; I don't have the strength or fortitude to be a pioneer." The ministry won, however, and she was ordained. Three years later, she left and taught in public school for a few years. "I wasn't satisfied, though; there was a definite sense of incompleteness, of not being where I should be or doing what I should be doing. I knew that I belonged in the parish ministry. After many months of correspondence (and despondence!), I was called to the church I now serve. In time I may move, but I'll stay in the ministry." [3]

Miss Spencer has homely advice for women aspirants to the clerical state: "Don't seek ordination on the basis of some romantic notion of being a peaceful pastor of a picturesque little white church on a hill, where your adoring congregation will flock to hear your words of wisdom on Sunday and cheerfully carry on a full and outgoing mission the rest of the week." (Exactly what picture the young aspirant is to keep in mind, however, Miss Spencer, perhaps out of prudence, does not say.)

Certainly no mercenary ambition influences a woman to leave nursing, teaching or business for the church, since only the smaller parishes are likely to be open to her. Yet some women accept uncertainty and financial insecurity in order to make that change. Why do they do it? "I was advised not to go into the ministry," another respondent admits. "My family opposed it; my pastor discouraged it and I myself did not *choose* to be a woman minister. This is something that happened in spite of me, something which I have never regretted but would never have attempted had I not felt that I *must*, that this was God's plan for me."

THE OTHER SIDE OF AGNOSTICISM

Several respondents in different age groups say that they entered seminary to find out if there were any answers to nagging spiritual questions too urgent to be postponed. A young, newly-ordained woman who is an assistant pastor explains that as a college student she lost the "simplistic, pietistic, inadequate, naive view of religion" with which she grew up. She sensed, however, that there was "a whole new world" in religion which she had never envisioned. "I went to seminary to explore this new world more thoroughly," not with the idea of becoming a minister. In fact she wanted to escape the attraction to religion: "I fervently wished I could be 'normal' and get married, rear a family and become involved in the routines and cycles of most women, but I was caught. I wanted to get away and yet I knew I couldn't. With graduation creeping up on me I was finally approached by several churches. I then decided that I could not, carte blanche, wipe out all churches, but must consider each church individually and each minister I would be working with"—and finally she became a Presbyterian minister.

I asked her if she would advise a college girl, with the attitude she had had, to go to seminary. She said, "My first inclination would be to discourage her, for I think this is a long and hard road to pursue. I would want to make sure that she did not picture the ministry as some rose-colored path; for I think seminary is hard on men as well as women. It is hard to be always wrestling with the 'ultimates' in life. However, on second thought, I would want to encourage her; for it is through this struggle that one becomes a whole person and finds those presuppositions upon which one can live, no matter whether she is a good wife and mother, or an ordained minister." She had been advised in college "not to take a second-rate Christian Education degree, but to go all the way. So I began a road that ended here, or rather, is only beginning here."

An ordained woman who teaches in college says, "I lost my faith in God at about age fourteen and subsequently wanted to help other young people avoid this painful and unnecessary experience." Adults with such motivation can doubtless do much to help young persons through the trying years when childhood religion seems hopelessly outmoded and there is as yet nothing valid to take its place. The vocabulary in which Christian experience is expressed quickly becomes antiquated. Words change their meaning as they pass from one generation to the next. If theological terms are made to seem more important than they are, meanings will escape from them, and the words falsify the very truths they are intended to keep intact. The living God cannot be locked up in semantic categories; he will break out every time, appearing in unexpected places. Faith is home-grown and cannot be imported across the generation gap. Perhaps it is by being persons of faith ourselves that we can best encourage others to hope that they, too, can struggle through to an honest and living experience of trust in God. Respondents Georgia Harkness and Rachel Henderlite, through their seminary teaching, writing and ecumenical work, are good examples of those who have long helped young persons with that struggle.

I interviewed one forthright young woman who told me she had been an atheist. Charmingly attired in a light suit, black blouse and clerical collar, she recalled, "I was a happy atheist who never attended church. I went to church, finally, because I was asked to sing. I wondered why people believed all this God-talk and read the entire New Testament to find out. That was the last step I took on my own initiative. By the time I finished the New Testament and some side reading, I was not only a convert to Christianity—I was a new person." When she went to seminary she had never made a public speech in her life and "tended to shun the spotlight." Today she is an ordained minister.

Those who have themselves known unbelief and later come to vital faith in God often bring to the ministry special sensitivity and sympathy for the problems of others.

CALLED THROUGH SUFFERING

Several of my respondents heard the call of God through suffering that seemed beyond endurance. The call they heard was not to patient resignation but to guided action. Viola Norman, a Methodist minister in Michigan, had such an experience. She recalls having a desire to become a minister when she was eight or nine years old, but was able to acquire only grammar school education. She married at the age of twenty-one; her first child lived only ten days. Later, she and her husband were able to adopt a baby boy, and subsequently, they had twin sons and another boy. Then, in the bewildering way tragedy sometimes singles out a family, both twins were killed instantly in an automobile accident, just before their nineteenth birthday, and their younger brother was critically injured.

In the midst of this torment, Mrs. Norman felt the presence of God as she sat in her surviving son's hospital room.

She felt uplifted and drawn to thanksgiving that this son was still living, even though the doctors had told her that he was beyond human help. She became conscious of a "mighty Voice" saying, "Go and give testimony of me, in any church of any denomination, wherever you are asked." Day after day, she felt the presence and heard the call. Finally, her son recovered.

I asked how her husband reacted to such a revelation. "A short time after God called me to preach," she answered, "my husband was awakened in the night by hearing his name called—'Dale.' I was sleeping and did not hear it, but he wakened me and I told him to go by himself and pray. He did, and God told him he was to go with me wherever I was called to preach, that we were to work together to help people in a meaningful ministry. We were both certain that we heard a voice, though it may have been with our spiritual ears. I don't think God gets through to us until we are ready to listen with faith." Today her husband, a retired mechanic, works with her.

When she approached the ministerial board of her district, they were naturally skeptical—grief can play strange tricks on the mind. The board tried to be helpful, however, and she began to study by correspondence. She also attended, for several years, a summer school for supply pastors, where she studied church history, worship, Christian education, theology, Bible, homiletics (preaching), and the sacraments. Because she did not have the educational background for such work, the director was surprised that she earned good grades. Mrs. Norman says, "I knew it was God who was giving me the strength and know-how; all I had to do was work very hard."

The first church to which she was sent as pastor had twenty-nine members. In a year's time, twenty-two more were received, "many of them eager young people." It was in this church that her younger son, who had been well five years, was married. Three and a half weeks later, after an illness of less than three days, he died. The day after the funeral, a brother minister preached for her but she taught her class of young people. "These youth needed to see our faith remain strong," she said. "Most of the class had tears in their eyes and our lesson turned into talk about eternal life."

Mrs. Norman has served small rural Methodist churches in Michigan for nearly twenty years. Her district superintendent calls her "energetic, hard-working, and consecrated," and she has permanent standing in the church as a local elder.

THE INNER VOICE

Psychologists point out [4] that, whereas men can have continuity in their pursuit of vocation, discontinuity usually characterizes the process of choice for a woman. Marriage and children affect the amount and kind of work she can do. It may be necessary for her to give up the position she held prior to motherhood, or, even if it proves possible for her to continue working outside her home, she may have to re-locate in a position more adaptable to her family situation. Then, later, as responsibilities lighten, she may be able to resume a more demanding type of work. In the meanwhile, her husband (fortunately for her) has been progressing steadily in his occupation. Only a serious family crisis normally forces discontinuity of choice upon a man.

This is the reality of the cultural situation as it has existed in our society, and as it still exists in many parts of the country. As has been noted, however, there are a growing number of exceptions to the traditional life patterns of women, especially in large metropolitan areas, but to follow one of them requires either courage or foolhardiness, depending on who is making the evaluation. Do women really wish to see the ideological changes that would compel them to work, as men do, through all the changing phases of their lives? Some women unavoidably face such necessity, but large numbers work because they want to, because they enjoy the freedom and additional income. Would they like to face the same legal requirements of family support men face?

Whatever answer women may give to this question in the future, it seems to me that the average woman must seek to understand the call of God in the light of her total situation today. With the full cooperation of her husband, and with family or other responsible help available, some young women are now carrying forward a successful ministry, even with several small children, without neglecting them or their own health. Not all who would like to follow this plan are able to do so, and society would rightly question the motivation of a woman who left a family of little children with strangers or persons not well known to her in order to give her time and energy to the ministry. A continuing urge "to preach the Gospel" might portend some future development in God's purpose for her, but should she not wait for a clarification of how the many needs of love are to be reconciled? The inner voice is never a weapon to be used for getting our own way without regard for others.

It is also worth remembering that a married man is never quite so free as some might consider him. It is true that he may often choose, prepare, enter and pursue his work without undue limitation, but many men are kept from occupations that appeal to them by poverty, early marriage, inability (for family reasons) to accept temporary insecurity, and other factors. Most single girls may act with considerable independence, but once a woman has assumed the responsibility of motherhood, the forms of her ministry may become unpredictably discontinuous. The responses to my questionnaire show flexibility and substantial change in the shape of ministry for married women. Denominational yearbooks find it hard to keep up with such changes and to classify them. It may sometimes appear that one who thinks she hears the call of God is deluded, but the situation is not relieved when men of any church, acting independently, try to prescribe the limits of woman's vocation.

Mary H. Ryan is a good example of a mature response to the possibility of woman's ministry in the present social context. Wife of a busy lawyer in Cleveland, Ohio, she served ten years as director of children's programs in the Camps Farthest Out, working with Glenn Clark, Rufus Mosely, Starr Daily, Glenn Harding, Frank Laubach, and others. The Camps Farthest Out are one of many predominantly lay spiritual life movements, interdenominational in character. Clergy are welcome to share in these camps, where Episcopal and Pentecostal people mingle with Methodists, Presbyterians, Baptists, and others, and non-church members also frequently attend. Ministers may participate in leadership but should expect no special recognition of status.

The idea of the Camps Farthest Out originated with Glenn Clark, a Presbyterian layman and one-time teacher at Macalester College in Minnesota. "When we received word of Glenn Clark's death at Council Ring at Lake Winnepesaukee, New Hampshire," Mrs. Ryan says, "something said to me, 'Now you must go into the ministry.'" Explaining her call further, she remarked, "A woman who has experienced a happy family life with four wonderful children grown to adulthood and all happily married, and nine grandchildren, can perhaps help younger families in their development and according to God's purpose."

Mrs. Ryan studied three years at Western Reserve University part time and completed her M. A. in Education, specializing in guidance counseling. Working as a director of Christian Education, she then took six years to complete her divinity studies, receiving her degree from Oberlin Graduate School of Theology.

Prior to seminary, Mrs. Ryan had taught in a juvenile detention home and at a house of correction for women. She had been assistant pastor of inner-city churches, also served in a suburban church while in seminary, and is now Minister of Education in an eastern suburb of Cleveland.

As the church becomes more accustomed to the ways of God's Spirit with women, many others may find a door opening to them where all the rich experience gleaned from motherhood and family life may be shared with the church and directed toward its mission. Kitchen and dining room are not the only places where women can work effectively for God. The domestic tasks that go on there are necessary, and may have special appeal for many; they are boring drudgery to others. Jesus did not send Mary of Bethany to the kitchen, even when pressed to do so; he approved her choice.

HEARING THE WORD

Some readers may remember a fantasy movie, *The Next Voice You Hear*, in which a divine voice interrupted and took over all radio broadcasts at a certain hour every evening for a week. Explanations were sought everywhere according to the preoccupations of the seekers: was there a scientific explanation? was it a publicity stunt engineered by a religious group? was it real? what was it? People dropped everything to listen while efforts were redoubled to discover the source. The content of the so-called word from God was about what one would expect—a combination of famous biblical passages and American idealism—but the amazing thing was the spirit I sensed among my fellow moviegoers themselves. There was a peculiar quietness as people left, almost a wistfulness, as though they were thinking, "How wonderful it would be if we could really know what life is all about but, of course, we never can." Similarly, Isak Dinesen has a character in one of her tales say, "If I had seen this little bit of bright color in the centerpiece [God's will for me], I would have understood the pattern, and would not have shaken it all to pieces so many times, and given the good Lord so much trouble in putting it together again."

Does anyone ever receive what appears to be, over the years, an authentic clue to personal existence? One cannot really speak for others, but such a clue was given to me when I was fifteen or barely sixteen years old. I was alone one night, praying. Although we lived on a noisy street, I became aware of a stillness that deepened into total silence. Into that silence came a penetrating, questioning impression that my mind groped for words to retain. Responding with willingness, but unable to do what was asked, I heard inwardly words of clarification and assurance that seemed to come from another. There was no sensory manifestation except the silence. Some days later, as I was reading the Bible, a passage penetrated as though spoken to me personally. It complemented what I had heard in prayer, and seemed to form, with that earlier event, a directive for my life, but neither the words I heard in prayer nor the biblical passage would have meaning in the setting of another person's experience. God, I believe, always accommodates himself to the "soul language" of the individual he addresses. It is not necessary to learn some special religious language in order to hear him.

In these early events there was no sense of being a specially chosen person. They seemed a normal occurrence such as anyone might encounter in prayer or Bible reading. They signaled no worthiness on my part, no insurance against future sin or mistakes, nor did they deliver me from ambiguities and obscurities to come.

When, in the process of education, I realized that comparable experiences had been studied by psychologists, I reflected further on the possible origin of what had taken place. It was easy to account, psychologically, for the fact that I had been praying and reading the Bible, but I could find no explanation for what was heard in prayer and illumined in the Bible.

These happenings were not isolated but have occurred, from time to time, over a period of many years. I have no idea as to how they might be induced, although they seem to take place, for the most part, within a context of prayer or worship, especially Holy Communion. What is heard is unpredictable and surprising. In the early years, the inner hearing seemed always to be followed, in a short time, by some strong biblical confirmation.

I have pondered C. G. Jung's experience (*Memories, Dreams, Reflections*) but, according to his own testimony, he had steeped himself in all kinds of mythological reading prior to receiving most of the messages from the Unconscious [5] that he found meaningful. In the first instances I was too young to have steeped myself in anything, but I acknowledge the *possibility* that in later experiences subliminally received suggestions from the Bible and elsewhere may have sprung into consciousness as though new.

Not until I was in seminary did I discover that the Hebrew language has a word for this kind of hearing. It is dābhār, and refers to a word from God that is also action, a word that does what it says, gives what it asks. This Hebrew word seemed to describe exactly what I had experienced, since what was conveyed was more than an intimation of the divine will: the word promised, encouraged, created, and called forth what I did not know was within me. [6]

In later years, I have noted that the word seems to bypass a need for memory, although it may be recalled. Human words are deposited in memory and brought back as occasion evokes them. The divine word becomes a building block in the personality and there is no need to recall it, for it is always present as an active element in experience. Wherever such a word has been preserved, in the Bible or elsewhere, it could never be defined or reduced to cold print; it is a seed that germinates in the receptive attention of someone capable of being helped by its special power. St. Jerome once remarked that God walks through the Bible. Of course, the Bible may be read as literature or studied in a scientific way with no possibility of divine intrusion whatever. But when a person, looking for God, goes persistently to its pages, it seems to me inevitable that, sooner or later, he will encounter the one he is seeking. One of our greatest difficulties today lies in a set of largely unexamined assumptions that has dulled popular expectation of help from such an ancient source.

This chapter should at least have shown that the origin of a sense of mission is mysterious beyond our present understanding. In any case, the call of God has come to women in many different ways. Their ministry, which we will consider in the next chapters, reflects what they have felt summoned to do.

3.

The Ministry of Single Women

Because society in general believes that the work a woman can do depends to a large extent upon her marital status, female ministry may perhaps be best discussed within that framework. My research shows that women have given careful thought to the service they can offer in the light of their obligations, and their ministry reveals a potential in womanpower that the church has scarcely begun to tap.

To Marry or Not to Marry

A Protestant man, looking toward the ministry, rarely faces this question. His contemporaries take for granted he will marry and hope he will have sense enough to pick a girl who will turn out to be a good minister's wife—whatever that is. A seminarian once asked a veteran of the cloth what kind of woman a prospective pastor ought to seek for a wife and was told, "One people will like."

The advisability of marriage itself, however, seems to be a crucial problem for attractive single women who, unattached, have reached the seminary stage of their education. Almost every man they meet in class shares, to some degree at least, their own goals. Will it be better for them to go on alone or, falling in love, can their ministry complement that of a husband? Is it possible to be an ordained minister and also a good wife and mother? A woman seminarian writes:

> One of the questions that is often raised by men in the ministry, and was also raised by my conference board, is the question of marriage. For myself, I do not find the ministry and marriage mutually exclusive. I have been dating several of the men in school here and feel that if I should marry one of them, I would have several alternatives: (1) shared ministry, (2) work in a neighboring church, (3) work as an area resource person, and (4) work in laboratory schools. Most important, though, is to find someone who is in sympathy with what you want to do and is active in the church himself.

This respondent, whose primary interest is education, has touched upon several problems raised by others.

Men do not usually want to marry women with education superior to their own, but in seminary a woman meets men of equal or higher education. Some of these men, of course, have traditional views of marriage and do not want their wives to be ministers at all, or only in a sense strictly complementary to their own work. A minister's success depends upon his relation to people; he feels that his home ought to be open to them and that a warm, friendly woman is needed there; he may not be able to visualize his wife at the beck and call of a different church, or having meetings of her own that would conflict with his schedule.

Suppose a woman seminarian loves such a man: what are her alternatives if she marries? It seems there are three: (1) re-conceiving her ministry in terms of homemaking (after all, homemaking, in a parsonage or elsewhere, is no small ministry in itself, although the church does not ordain for this purpose); (2) serving her husband's church without pay, and with or without professional status, in a manner complementary to his work; or (3) entering with her husband the service of a church large enough to pay two salaries. With regard to the first alternative, a woman graduating from seminary has, by the very fact, departed from one traditional role expectation of her sex—she has prepared to engage in a profession. This does not preclude loving a man deeply and becoming a good wife and mother, but she will bring to homemaking additional understanding and insight that will enable her to find areas of service outside the usual homemaking tradition; these can be both an opportunity for ministry and personal fulfillment. As for the third alternative, there are at present few churches willing to take on the responsibility of paying a salary to both husband and wife, especially when they can get talented, active ministers' wives free! The second option is most promising, although it implies a woman can handle homemaking and a career without much domestic help. At this juncture, a single ministerial salary (except in the highest brackets, seldom open to seminary graduates in their early years) would be inadequate.

The happiness of a woman preparing for the ministry (or for any significant work outside her own home) depends upon marrying a man who is "in sympathy with what she wants to do," or remaining single. Unfortunately, there are not enough liberal husbands to go around, and a woman preparing for a career has only a fifty-fifty chance of meeting one.

Two respondents, as they explored their interests in greater depth with men to whom they had become engaged, discovered that marriage was impossible for them. One says, "He could not share my sense of calling." The other experienced an increasing conflict of values and, after a struggle, decided that marriage would have been a "tempting escape" for her.

Could such an attitude be understood as a "call to celibacy," somewhat in the Roman Catholic pattern? The several unmarried women with whom I discussed this question vehemently denied any similarity. First, they feel that the Catholic pattern implies that those who decide against marriage are following a higher vocation. Most of my respondents, on the contrary, have no sense of superiority, and many of them think the married state would be preferable if it combined the freedom to minister with the understanding and support of a husband—and without pressure to conform to stereotyped assumptions of what a married woman ought to do.

Such women live a day at a time, neither ruling out the possibility of marriage nor desiring it at any price—they are open to life as it comes. Some believe they would not be unfaithful to their call if they were to marry and partially withdraw from the ministry for a number of years to have children and see them into school; they would then return to service. In addition, half a dozen respondents married happily late in life; but two others, now past sixty, reveal they chose early in life and did not alter that decision. One says, "I never married because I felt the ministry needed my entire time and service. This was the hardest decision I ever made, for I had domestic tastes and loved children very much. As pastor and woman, however, I have cared for newborn babies, raised them in my churches in a mission field, married them when they were grown; some now have children named after me, so I have joy in 'my family.'" The other writes, "Certainly, God's plan is for marriage. In my case, I felt he wanted me to give my full time to him. I am for marriage but felt I should obey the inner urge to make this dedication of myself."

Several young women say that they would not have the stamina to combine ministry and homemaking. "I can't imagine being a married woman and remaining in the active ministry, at least, not in a pastorate. I would find raising a family quite ministry enough," says one. The opinion of another is: "Personally, I am not a well enough organized person to be able to run a household, care for kids, and serve a church adequately. Maybe this is my problem. But for me, I'm sure it would have to be either/or."

This point of view, on the part of a *woman*, which seems to put ministry before marriage, may be hard for Protestants to understand. In our reaction against Catholic monasticism we have so glorified marriage as the one possibility of fulfillment for a woman that single persons are often made to feel they have missed the meaning of life. Several unmarried women (not ministers) have, in fact, told me, "The church is the place of my deepest loneliness." Is this degree of emphasis on marriage as the only fulfillment either helpful or sound? Roman Catholics seem to have made their mistake in the opposite direction by glorifying celibacy. Even among the Orthodox, the priest who has chosen to marry has removed himself from the possibility of becoming a bishop. Have we not all made a person's state in life the prime consideration, instead of leaving men and women free to put ministry first, leaving their state in life as a subordinate personal option?

This option involves ramifications for women, however, that men do not have to face. Usually the more education a man receives, the more desirable he becomes as a candidate for marriage; the opposite may be true for women. "Being a minister puts up barriers against eligibility for dating in many men's minds," says one respondent. "A young fellow in the youth program of the church," writes another, "told his girl friend that he could never marry a minister. When his girl friend asked him why, and reminded him that I was a minister, he couldn't find any real reason; it was just a feeling." There is the possibility, then, that single life, while not consciously chosen, may result from a woman's desire to become a minister.

Jesus advised his followers to "count the cost" before starting to build, rather than rush blindly into projects they could not finish. While I was in college, an ordained woman past middle age shared an intimate part of her life with me, knowing that I planned to enter the service of the church. When I expressed admiration for the way in which she seemed able to rise above all visible frustrations, enjoying men and women equally, she confided in me:

> I began preaching as a very young person, completely absorbed in the work. The thought of marriage never crossed my mind. Then suddenly, in my thirties, I brought my eyes down from heaven long enough to notice the way husbands looked at their wives, and to watch the expression on women's faces as they cuddled their babies. A black shadow fell over me which I could not push away. I became bitter toward God. I had cared for nothing except his kingdom but he had shown no corresponding concern for my interests. An important part of life had simply passed me by. It took some time to emerge from this darkness, and then it was only through the grace and goodness of God. Since that period, I see human beings in a different light.

I asked an aged single woman, whose long, productive pastoral service was well known to me, what she would say on this subject to a college girl aspiring to the ministry. She replied:

> Is she willing to forego marriage for the sake of the ministry? If she is fortunate enough to establish a home with a seminarian or one already established in the ministry, excellent. She will find opportunity to render most effective service in assisting her husband. But if she should marry

a man in another profession or in a certain type of business that requires that he live in a particular area, what happens if she or her church finds that her services are no longer needed in that place? No church is going to call a minister with a "life lease" arrangement. Moreover, every man wants to be a success in his profession. Nor does he want to be known merely as "Reverend Mrs. So and So's husband."

Is this response dated, or does it still have validity? Men are increasingly hospitable to the idea that their wives should have the chance to be persons in their own right, yet even today few could accept identification in terms of their wife's profession. Those secure in their masculinity and competent in their own work can face a temporary situation of this kind, but many men would be threatened beyond acceptance.

One aspect of the picture is changing, however, in that more than fifty specialized ministries are developing.[1] If a woman can fulfill her call in one of these, marriage may be possible without threat to the average man's happiness. Writing, for example, can be done in one's own home. Can this not be a proclamation of the word? There are ministerial functions which can be carried out in controlled blocks of time. A combination of ordained ministry and marriage may be more feasible for women in the near future than even in the recent past.

WORKING WITH DENOMINATIONAL LEADERS

While some persons seem disposed to bypass the institutional church, the vast majority of Christians remain in it, trying to work with the system as best they can, changing it from within. And can we be sure that those leaving one institution will not create another, even less adequate, to take its place? Unless a woman wants to be known as a rebel, with all that entails, she will have to learn how to deal with denominational officials, most of whom are men. Does this pose any special problem for the single woman? Perhaps, indirectly, it does.

Some years ago, a single woman minister told me tartly, "Never get the idea that it is the Lord who fights your battles for you; it is not; it is your husband." Taking a fresh look at my husband from this new angle, I could see she was right. He had certainly smoothed the way in the beginning by arranging for my examination and ordination along with his own. While I had not wanted a professional relationship to the church of which he was pastor, he had always recognized my ministry, inviting me to preach occasionally, and to share, as far as time and energy permitted, in projects that interested me, such as leadership education. His attitude opened the door to acceptance on the part of other ministers and churches, so that supply and interim preaching, as well as interdenominational work, were a natural outgrowth. While single women can offer time and mobility, married women often have a more ready access to certain forms of ministry through their husbands. In interviews, several single women mentioned that marriage adds to a woman's status and makes contacts with men easier.

If their assessment is true, how can a single woman establish a good relationship with those who will help to make future pastoral work possible for her? We mention this area of service first because the local church has been the central witnessing community in the past; it remains strongly entrenched, with buildings, personnel and money; and, despite social change, it is likely to be with us for a long time. Ordained ministry is still defined, to a considerable extent, in terms of "word and sacrament." New patterns, to be discussed later, do not obviate this fact.

It seems to me a girl is wise not to allow seminary to become a parenthetical expression in her life. Try as they may to meet diversified needs of students, seminaries are academic institutions with high requirements. It is possible, while there, to let walls of scholarship shut out the world, even though one may be doing regular field work. Long-range personal goals may be dimmed by the necessities of the current year's study. Away from her local church and denominational leaders who are responsible for her, a girl may become careless about keeping in touch, fail to answer correspondence, and allow people with whom she has had introductory contacts to forget about her existence. This may indicate to others an indifference she does not feel.

It would seem the better course for the seminary student to get acquainted from the outset with the nearest offices of her church, to attend denominational meetings, and to keep in touch with developing programs. While visions of changing patterns are alluring, in all too brief a time a student will face the reality of having to secure a place to work. Unless she has abundant financial resources, she will make the painful discovery that most highly lauded experimental ministries are still rather nebulous, and that she must continue to await her opportunity with the aid of the institutional church.

This situation is more poignant where a woman is concerned, because placement takes longer. If she has been in a liberal seminary, free from prejudice against her sex, the delay will be disillusioning. She may feel that denominational leaders are hostile or indifferent. If they are not, she asks herself, where is the bottleneck?

Undoubtedly there are still individual men in high positions who would like to avoid the problems involved in the placement of women pastors, but in those churches which have decided to ordain women most officials are willing to help. Respondents give an all but uniformly favorable report on their relationships with bishops, district superintendents, conference ministers, and those in similar positions. An able woman, summarizing her professional relationship with men, says,

> Both in the Congregational churches and in the ecumenical work, I found, with a few notable exceptions, my most appreciated support from men who were themselves at the top level. When local male colleagues were nice, they were very, very nice, but some of them *could* be horrid. With younger men it took the form of professional rivalry; some older ministers were outspoken in their opposition, on theological grounds, to women ministers.

This is the evaluation of nearly all the women who offered comments on the subject: helpful support from denominational officials, a good relationship with most male clergy, but some unpleasant experiences with a minority of them.

This picture is not peculiar to any one or two denominations. Those engaged in the Consultation on Church Union have been growing toward each other, even structurally, for a number of years.

In all these churches, women who seek a pastoral ministry have come to realize that their sex is a liability. Not only does initial placement take longer, but moving is more difficult for them. When such problems can be discussed with a husband, frustration and uncertainty are reduced considerably. A wife can be jollied into laughing at her fears. She can be teased into better humor when irritated by delays. Her financial situation is not threatening. An evening's recreation can restore her sense of balance. Both single and married women point out that it takes much more courage to face depressing doubts alone.

Perhaps the most important thing to remember here is to avoid self-pity. When a church leader discovers that a woman is patient, understanding and appreciative of his efforts, that she will not dissolve into tears or recriminations, he will usually do his best for her. Her ministerial record will be presented again and again—not with those of men who have the same ability she has, it is true (otherwise, she might never be accepted), but with men of somewhat less ability, until a church, recognizing that capacity for ministry is more important than sex, gives her a chance. There are such forward-looking parishes. As a respondent says, "If God calls, and we keep ourselves in a relationship of love toward both him and our fellow human beings, our future is in his hands. A way will open." The best recommendation a woman (or man) can have, when it comes to moving, is a record of solid accomplishment resulting from hard work. "Every statistic represents a person who has been reached and brought into the fellowship of the church," says one denominational leader. This may be optimistic but there is a kernel of truth in it.

Is Ordination a Rights Issue?

Ordination usually follows initial placement but, if problems regarding that placement multiply, a woman may be tempted to bitterness and become militant about her "rights." Denominational officials frequently find it hard to assist her in moving to positions offering larger opportunities, while men with less ability pass her easily.

Opinions as to whether or not ordination is a right for which women should contend differ among female clergy themselves. Marie Hubbel, who has been a pastor in California and is now doing graduate work, tells ordained women, "Never, for whatever provocation, take up the cause of women's rights. For us to espouse this cause is to lose friends and influence." Miss Hubbel thinks discrimination is "in the nature of things" and unintentional. "We are oddities and have to expect a certain amount of wariness among clergy and laity. But for all that, we are ministers of God . . . and can give thanks for our place." [2]

Militancy on the part of a woman minister places men on the defensive. Their reaction may be a combination of semi-guilt over an unfair situation they feel personally power-less to remedy and irritation with the woman for making a fuss about what cannot be helped. The issue is similar to that of civil rights; there is an additional difficulty in that relationships between men and women are even more com-plicated and delicate than those between races. Waging a feminist war and serving a local parish do not mix well. Tilda Norberg, a young respondent, writes, "I feel that what is called for is not women's rights as such, but a whole reor-dering of male-female relationships, so that we act out of a commitment to the development of real personhood in both men and women, rather than out of traditional role mod-els." This approach calls for the re-education of adults so that the atmosphere of home life, and eventually of social life, can be changed. But is this too slow a process?

Quite a few will say it is, for females do face crippling discrimination when they attempt to dedicate their gifts to God through the church. Perhaps some will feel drawn to militancy in this regard. Numbers count, and they may feel let down by what appears to be indifference on the part of those who should join forces with them. Do their meeker sisters want to reap the benefits of feminist work without facing its hardships? This point of view is understandable but it seems to me that men can do more for women in this regard than women can do for themselves. If, for example, a man believes he has received a real call to ministry, how can he face God in prayer and deny a woman the privilege of responding to the same invitation? I believe that the great majority of Christian men will defend women in their desire to serve God, once they grasp the spiritual import of what is being asked. Countless men have already come to the defense of women, urging them toward ordination.

A far deeper question, however, is pertinent here. If ordi-nation is the action of the church in response to God's call to individuals, it can scarcely be treated as a right by either sex, can it? But even if it were a right, is not our proper concern within the church the rights of others rather than insistence upon our own? If the call to ministry is seen to be a gift of grace, should not women go about their own business, ministering the best they can, while men, forgetting the common estimate of women and studying the graces of ministry given to them, undertake to secure for women what is willed by God? A woman's chief responsibility, then, would be to try to make clear to men within the church what she feels her call to be. Can she not, then, trust men to do their best to help her?

Power struggles, though constantly invading (and corrupting) the visible church, do not belong in the Christian family. It may be a vocation in itself for women to fight for their rights in the secular world but the ministry is another matter. Until human brotherhood is, in fact, reached, is not the church called to be an outgoing family within society?

In this same connection, however, is it not a matter of some importance to the church that women, called by God, should be able to establish their true identity within its fellowship? The spiritual identity of a married woman may be obscured by society's long habit of seeing her in terms of husband and children. What identity does a single woman have, when she believes herself called by God to ministry, if the church refuses to recognize her? I shall return to this question in the last chapter.

Supportive Roles for Women?

If a woman's sense of call can be given valid response through a supportive or specialized service on a multiple staff, she will have a much easier time, since she will then be conforming to traditional biblical anthropology which sees woman as helper to man. This status is congenial to many respondents who prefer to be assistants or associates of male clergy. A single woman who occupies a high post in the educational ministry of the church summarizes what others have expressed:

> I would personally rather be an associate minister with the function of Christian education if I were in a local parish; this happens to be my specialization, and I do not care for full administrative responsibilities. It takes a woman of special personality and ability to be the minister in charge of a local parish, but I have known many who were very effective here. I would just plead for an openness to the person's qualifications regardless of sex. Let me add that since I did not aspire to be a parish minister or a chief executive officer in an organization, I have not felt my sex to be a particular handicap in my professional work. Had I had either of these aspirations and abilities, however, I'm sure I would have encountered the problem of not being chosen for the position I was capable of because of my sex. I have really sensed little progress in this area—in fact, women in executive positions are fewer now than several years ago because of the trend toward consolidation of women's departments within the total work of the church.

The plea "for an openness to the person's qualifications" comes from many respondents. Very few, even among those who prefer supportive positions, want to see their sex *stereotyped* for them. This point is of special importance to single women, who are usually free to locate where they wish and do not have to consider other persons in the use of their time. This raises the question: if they are intellectually creative, why should they subordinate themselves to male leadership and always hold a secondary place?

The root problem is biblical and might be posed in this way: is the subordination of woman to man a part of revelation, or a characteristic of the social setting in which revelation occurs, or are the two so interwoven that the effort to separate them would destroy revelation itself? I once asked a nurseryman how to get asparagus out of my rose garden and he advised me to let it stay, as I might damage the roses. There are those who have the same view of trying to isolate revelatory material from the mass of geographical, biographical and sociological data in the Bible.

The question is serious for the church at many levels. I am concerned here about the way selected biblical passages are used to limit the work of women in the church. Take, for example, I Corinthians 14:34-5, where Paul (if it is Paul [3]) unequivocally states, "The women should keep silence in the churches . . . it is shameful for a woman to speak in church." If one is looking for proof that women should not preach, clearly this is evidence for that position. In the light of modern scholarship, however, such argumentation is simplistic.

First, how is Paul's statement to be reconciled with I Corinthians 11:5 and 13, where it is taken for granted that women will be praying and prophesying in public worship? Only by speculative worrying of these texts can they be raised above contradictory meanings.

But more important is the fact that today we do not attempt to interpret any biblical passage without careful attention to the situation with which it deals. The Christians in Corinth, to whom this letter is addressed, were recent converts from paganism. Every form of immorality flourished in their city and they had not been untouched by it. Public credence was given to any wild tale about what went on at Christian "love feasts." No one could have been more eager than Paul for women to reap the full benefit of their liberation in Christ but he did not want the church to get a bad reputation by socially irresponsible behavior based on poor judgment.

The problem Paul faced was as hard to solve as the current dilemma of downtrodden groups as to how they may secure justice without violent revolution. Many Christians struggle with the same ambivalence on this issue that Paul faced with regard to freedom for women. His conservative education in Jewish law prompted him to be very strict about feminine reticence and yet he knew that Jesus had not discriminated between the sexes. We can see the struggle going on in his mind in I Corinthians 11:7ff., where he states the accepted Jewish view of male superiority and then continues, "In the Lord woman is not independent of man nor man of woman; for as woman was made from man, so man is now born of woman. And all things are from God." Immediately, however, he brings to mind what is "proper," what "nature itself" teaches (points which in our day would be considered sociological and psychological), tossing the question back and forth in an effort to evolve useful directives for the church. (Remember I Corinthians is not a studiously prepared essay but a rapidly dictated letter.) When we are able to recognize that the early Christians were not supermen who had all the answers but human beings like ourselves, trying to put what they learned from Jesus into practice, their example will no longer bind the church but free it to relate to an ever-changing culture.

In this connection, it is interesting to note the attitude of women in Pentecostal Churches, because these churches strongly emphasize fidelity to the literal interpretation of the Bible and, at the same time, retain tremendous faith in what the Holy Spirit says to and through the living person. These women, conscious of their own call, turn instinctively to what the apostle Paul says in his letter to the Galatians, "There is neither male nor female for you are all one in Christ Jesus." [4] They do not, however, reject passages commanding the subordination of women, and accept the idea that the husband is to be the authority in a family. In practice, this does not distinguish them as much as might be supposed from families where parents are regarded as joint authorities. An elderly Pentecostal respondent told me that a young husband in her church wanted to make her arbitrator between himself and his wife, whom he did not consider properly submissive. She did not question for a moment his male prerogatives but asked him to read further in the fifth chapter of Ephesians for better insight into his own role of unselfish love. "If you do your part there," she counseled him soberly, "you will have your wife eating out of your hand." Just as the directives given to slaves and masters in the New Testament, when obeyed, created a climate in which slavery was no longer tenable, so instructions to husbands and wives, when followed faithfully, create a home life in which the question of relative authority ceases to be significant.

The same principle applies to the church. Where Christian love exists, the talents and training of both sexes can be given full scope without male "authority" becoming a touchy issue.

Women enjoy teamwork with men and supportive roles might prove more attractive to them if certain hardships were faced realistically. A young Presbyterian woman, happy as an assistant pastor, feels that assistants (men as well as women) should "be installed by Presbytery rather than by session. As it is now, an assistant must depend upon the support of the senior pastor to protect him or her in terms of continued employment. It might be well if all assistants were made associates since associates have the same protection and status in Presbytery as senior pastors." Security is as important to a woman as to a man. Another, who thinks that "positions of leadership for women in the Presbyterian Church are narrowing," points out that women in supportive positions are the first to be eliminated when economies become necessary. Those who "labor outside the bounds of Presbytery" might not have chosen to do so had the church realized more fully the nature of their problems within the structure.

A few respondents point out imbalance of salary, one United Church of Christ woman minister reporting, "The major obstacle has probably been financial—never once have I received more than about half of what was paid to the 'man' minister, though, except for one man, I had higher earned degrees in all cases."

IN THE LOCAL CHURCH

When she begins work in a local parish accustomed to male clergy, a woman runs into incredulity at every turn: "I have never met a lady minister before; are you for real?" The "lady minister" reports, "I felt as though I should produce two heads or perform like a trick bear." The novelty will soon wear off, however, as she goes about her work in a matter-of-fact way.

Getting acquainted. Time and mobility, as we have noted, are two important assets which a single woman minister can offer to the church, but she is only one person. A family in the parsonage goes out into the community at as many levels as there are children. With no one of her own to care for and to limit the geographical boundaries of her service, the single woman is free to make the church her family to whatever extent she desires. Occupying the parsonage home alone, she has no one else to consider in the use of it, but getting started may be hard. One young pastor, trying to get close to the people in her first parish, confided to her Methodist district superintendent, "I just can't seem to get acquainted with them. I feel so on the outside." Looking around at the tastefully furnished home and back into her eager eyes, he inquired, "Have you thought of entertaining groups of them here?" That they might like to be invited into her home had not occurred to her. Some women ministers pride themselves on being good cooks and enjoy entertaining parishioners. People seeing the pastor only in the church may come to think of her as part of the equipment. One respondent was met in the supermarket by a church member who asked, "What are you doing here?" She replied that she liked to cook and eat too!

When parishioners entertain a minister in their own homes, children develop a different attitude toward the pastor as a person. The artless remarks of children at the dinner table may also enlighten the clergy. A respondent, asked to say grace in such a setting, evidently took considerably longer than the father of the family. When she finished, the small son emitted a sigh and said, *"Phew,* that was a long talk!" (She remembered the incident when, many years later, he called her from another state to baptize his baby.) The informality of having guests and being a guest opens doors to deeper levels of communication.

Working with men. The average Protestant minister finds his wife a great help with the women of the church. She keeps him posted on the feminine viewpoint as it is expressed in women's meetings and elsewhere. The single woman has no such assistant in her work with men but, if the church is to be a force for good in the community, it is imperative that she have a cooperative relationship with them. How does she manage this?

I asked a woman who has a record of successful church administration. She said it had never presented any special problem to her. She sought expressions from her church cabinet (both men and women) as to their understanding of the mission of the church in the community. They explored mutual insights regarding local needs and, of course, they were hearing her sermons on Sunday mornings. "People volunteer for various tasks and I anticipate their taking responsibility in an adult manner for things they say they will do. I dictate neither to men nor to women. It is dictatorial women, I think, whom men resent, not women performing an obvious task of pastoral leadership."

No woman among my correspondents found working

with male parishioners frustrating. In fact, most seem to believe that there is less friction in this phase of their work than male clergy experience. Some feel that women are better listeners, less inclined to be impatient for quick results, less patronizing in their relationship with the laity. One who has given many years to a form of denominational educational work that brings her into close contact with a wide variety of lay persons stresses the importance of their being heard; they want to express and discuss their views on many issues. One time a man asked her if her listening and encouragement of lay participation was "a new trend in the church" or "just *your* way."

The pastor of a church slightly above average in membership provided additional insight: "I must confess that I probably worked a little harder to interest and enthuse men in various areas of service within the church, because in most instances it was the women who were doing practically everything. And I am of the strong conviction that just as a home needs both a father and a mother, so the church needs both men and women. This had been a woman's church—they held all the offices. I recall being rather bold at the first meeting of one of the commissions after one of the women flatly asserted that no man would be willing to serve on it. I quickly replied, 'Maybe they haven't been given the chance,' and we began to draft men to various positions (which, of course, can't be done unless they are willing to be drafted)." This pastor clearly has the firm support of men in her congregation. She has steered three churches through successful building programs but says, "I would have been happy to leave that job to the men!"

One element that may enter into the success of women pastors in working with men is that the average man assumes a woman pastor needs his help. Male clergy, on the other hand, can look out for themselves and find someone else to do a hard job.

Counseling. One might suppose that single women would find it perplexing to counsel the married, but though some see this as a problem, the majority do not. Assessments like the following, from a woman pastor in Missouri, were frequent:

> A woman has the advantage of being able to wander into another woman's kitchen during the day, staying for a cup of tea, lunch, or what have you, and in so doing, serve as counselor without formally counseling. I think the woman minister is aware of some of the more intricate relationships in family living because of her less formal contacts with women in the congregation. When I was in a dual situation, men were just as likely to consult me as they were to consult the male minister.

Counseling in average or smaller churches is usually quite informal and parishioners may often talk with a young, single woman about matters which they think she may have studied or with which she may have had some experience during her years of preparation. Even in large city parishes, counseling may come about in the ordinary routine work of the church. A young, single director of Christian education in a large city church, who made it a practice to have long yearly interviews with each person on her teaching staff, observed that men as well as women would frequently discuss personal problems with her because they were interested in the point of view of a trained woman who could see their situation objectively.

Most respondents believe that individual differences count more heavily in ministering to human need than differences of sex. Obviously, sex closes certain doors: women ministers cannot fraternize with men at Lions Club or Kiwanis and men ministers cannot "help the bride dress, even in an emergency," as one respondent puts it. A female pastor in a Southern state comments:

One of my colleagues in this town recently asked me to counsel with a young woman in his church, because he felt a woman could do better with her than a man could do (and this minister does not believe that women should be pastors!). On the other hand, there is a man who attends my church that I have never been able to get close enough to because there are just no natural opportunities for us to be alone together and have the kind of talk that pastor and parishioner need to have. (His wife is so eager for him to join the church that she tells me when and where I might be able to find him alone, but it never seems to work out!)

On the whole, the individual, whether male or female, will minister out of whatever personal resources are possessed without regard to sex. Normal pastoral relationships require ability to help people who face ordinary problems and to recognize disturbances which have progressed to the point that referral to other professions is needed. Many women today, however, are preparing or have prepared to give highly specialized ministries.

BEYOND THE LOCAL CHURCH

As has been seen, the largest single group of respondents experience their strongest attraction to pastoral work, including preaching. While Christian education appeals to many, relatively few want to be confined exclusively to this area. Hence we have the peculiar situation that women find the least initial acceptance in the work which appeals to them most.

This fact, well known to seminary advisers, creates a problem: when a woman has consecrated her life to God and obviously has gifts the church needs, what counsel can one give? Where is she to preach if the local church does not call her? Where can her love and care for others find most fruitful expression? A woman who is now teaching in college says that the president of her large Eastern seminary "told me that I would have more satisfying opportunities to preach (as a guest) if I became a college professor than if I went into the parish ministry. Supplying for student pastors or administering the sacraments in churches served by those not yet ordained can accompany teaching religion." (All of the seminary professors and half of the college professors among respondents are single women.) Another college professor who fought against the oddity of being a minister but was urged toward ordination by the dean of her seminary said that her counselors seemed to think "I should find a rich pastoral ministry on the college campus, and I must say I have. Chaplains are usually men but both men and women at times need a woman for consultation, confession and reassurance." There seems to be as strong a pastoral motivation in the women doing higher educational work, or holding state or national posts in education, as in those serving the local church. Once the initial difficulty in securing a position has been surmounted, they are well received and valued for the contribution they make as faculty advisers or executives.

It is impossible to guess how many women turn away from professional service of the church, however, because of prejudice against their leadership at the local level. An incident which occurred on an Eastern seminary campus, where orientation to church-related vocations was being given to college women, was relayed to me. Subtle but pervasive emphasis upon supportive or specialized roles for women conveyed the strong impression to the girls that they were not wanted as pastors of local churches. Following the meeting, a young woman remarked to a friend, "If this is the lay of the land in the church, I am going into medicine."

The more talent a woman has, the more oppressive she

finds the low ceiling of possibility for professional development within the church. She may feel quite literally pushed off its salary rolls into a specialized ministry under the auspices of another institution. One young woman minister, structured out of an excellent position in a supportive role, saw four possibilities for her future: to become a rural pastor, a director of religious education, a dean of women in a church-related school, or a director of a specialized ministry in an institution friendly to the church. She chose the last as offering the best scope for her talents and abilities. This has not meant "leaving the ministry," because she has had about the same opportunity for preaching the word and administering the sacrament (Holy Communion), either denominationally as guest or ecumenically, as she had before leaving the employ of the institutional church. But what kind of image of the church do multiplying incidents of such limited choice give to women?

Miss Barbara Troxell, now working with the YWCA on Stanford University campus in California, began as a pastor, but still has opportunity for the administration of the sacrament. She sees this "as a kind of culmination of the ministry of healing, of pastoral care, of preaching, and of prophetic witness-bearing. It is at the Eucharist that all the other functions are gathered up into a celebrative act of the re-membering (that hyphen is important!) of the body of Christ." While her ordination is not highlighted in her present on-campus service, she is glad to be ordained because there is continuing possibility for a sacramental ministry.

Specialization may come about in quite unpredictable and surprising ways. Several critically handicapped women are among my respondents, some married, some single. Miss Virginia Kreyer says, "From the time I was a teen-ager I felt that I could render the greatest service and would find the greatest happiness in a church-related vocation. Later, I became absolutely convinced that this was God's will for my life." She shared her purpose with others and was encouraged to pursue it. Then the struggle began:

> Between my sophomore and junior years in college, I began to question seriously how I, a person born with cerebral palsy and whose greatest disability was speech, could enter a vocation in which the ability to communicate through the spoken word was so important. Reluctantly I gave up my cherished dream and decided, with my parents' urging, to open a card and gift shop. When I returned to college that September and told my major professor (English) of my decision, she let me know that she could not agree. Besides pointing out that many who had tried to open gift shops had failed, she said she believed I would be wasting my talents. I was a little upset but very relieved.

A few weeks later, at a church service, the guidance of her teacher was confirmed inwardly in a pronounced way.

During her first year at seminary, she asked a man who held a high executive church office if he felt there would be a place of service following her graduation. His honest but jolting reply was, "I just don't know." A few days later at a chapel service, she felt again the strong inner confirmation: "There is a place of service for you. You must complete your seminary training and never again question my call."

The years following her graduation were difficult. She did not always feel that her theological training was being put to use. She had been ordained for a special ministry with the United Cerebral Palsy Association of Nassau County, New York, and, for a time, was Acting Director of the Social Service Department during a staff shortage, having also received her master's degree in social work. There were times when it was hard for her to understand the relationship between what she was doing and ministry as she had always conceived it. She writes:

Now, however, with the new theological understanding of ministering in the secular world, I realize that what I have been doing is indeed a ministry. Most of our generation grew up with the feeling that if one was to be a minister in a "church-related vocation," that work had to be carried on within the confines of the organized church. It took me a long time to reach the point where I could accept the fact that I was ministering in Christ's name (or rather His Spirit), as I counseled with the handicapped and their families, even though I never referred to Christ and the church. In other words, we don't have to use his name to minister in his Spirit.

In 1957, the National Council of Churches sponsored a Consultation on Exceptional Persons at Green Lake, Wisconsin. From that meeting a Council Committee on the Christian Education of Exceptional Persons developed in 1959. Miss Kreyer served on that committee, which gave new importance to four areas of work—with the physically handicapped, the mentally retarded, the emotionally disturbed, and those in custody. While the committee no longer functions as such, curricula for some of these groups are now being prepared.

Miss Kreyer is an American Baptist; as a result of her master's thesis in social work, investigating the extent of physical disability and mental retardation in her denomination, a staff person has been hired in that field, and a group home for the retarded was begun. In addition, several Union Seminary students have done field work in the County Home for the Aged under chaplaincy supervision, and in cerebral palsy under Miss Kreyer's supervision. One student summed up his feelings, "If I had never visited the center, I would not have been forced to face the problem of evil seriously, to consider why God allows people to bear disabilities, some of which are very severe."

Has Miss Kreyer abandoned entirely the ministry of word and sacrament? She still preaches occasionally and friends have told her that when she does so, her speech becomes crystal clear. She attributes this to the power of God alone, working through her.

THE PERENNIAL PROBLEM

The greatest single hardship of the unmarried seems to be a very human loneliness which increases over the years, present even when one has spiritual resources to cope with it. Kindhearted lay persons fear a young woman may be lonely and move to counteract this, sometimes failing to give her sufficient leisure for herself, but as women grow older, people may give little thought to their depressing sense of being without a family. Invitations to Sunday dinners and holiday gatherings cannot dispel the awareness of loss. One respondent, who pointed out that single women of other professions, and also widows, face the same loneliness, and that it can be even more acute for the married if there is no depth of understanding between the partners, nevertheless writes:

> They think we wouldn't want to come to a party to play games or engage in controversial conversation. I'd like to go to a party where the men are not in a separate room discussing cattle and the women in the kitchen comparing recipes, but where all are in the same room, mixed up together, talking together about something besides "shop", or playing games together. Single women would like to listen to men and talk to them about politics, social action or just gay repartee. We miss this. Family nights at the church are not social events for the single woman preacher. In fact, she has no social life and something should be done about this.

Other correspondents suggest that, in loneliness, a woman is tempted to take herself too seriously, to overwork, and to become intense about it. "You need someone you can trust and to whom you can explode when tensions build up." But most of those who answered my question about the advantages and disadvantages of single life would agree, I think, with this assessment:

> As a single person, one has to be willing to dare to love deeply with the realization that parting may be more frequent, and that no family core of love and concern can be taken with you. The hurt could be far more devastating unless one were willing to establish new roots just as deep in another place at another time.

But is singleness itself so remote from the common path that those who go that way, of necessity, speak another language, and is being a woman one additional barrier to communication between pulpit and pew? A small Oklahoma town was shaken by the news that it would soon find out; the next Methodist pastor would be a girl undertaking her first charge. Unnerved by the news, a member went out to weed her garden and ponder the plight of the church: "I had asked the good Lord to send us a fine preacher, and he is sending a *woman*. Then I got to thinking—I had not specified male or female." [5] Perhaps the good Lord to whom she appealed did not think it mattered as long as his word was heard and his love shown.

4.

The Ministry of Married Women

Protestants are convinced that a good marriage furthers a man's ministry. They hope to have husband, wife, and a few children in the parsonage. The children should be well behaved—not the type who write on wallpaper or leave their toys to trip unsuspecting parishioners attending a meeting at the manse. Neither should offspring be so plentiful as to require exorbitant increases in ministerial salaries. It is hard to visualize a young, single woman in a large parsonage, however, and it is even more difficult to contemplate a married woman trying to serve a church. Hasn't the latter left the ministry for the career of wife and mother?

Conservative sectors of society want to keep wives at home, or in volunteer work, unless economic pressure forces them out to earn a living. Isn't it the task of the church, they reason, to preserve traditional values? Should not a religious woman set an example by centering her life in her family? Her husband has a right to expect it; so does the church. Despite social change, many people still find it impossible to accept the premise that a wife may have responsibility beyond her role as mother and homemaker. From their point of view, a woman who tries to be both a homemaker and a minister will end by being neither. Is this position tenable as we approach the twenty-first century, or can ordained women who marry serve beyond their homes without failing their families? We will look first at ministers' wives.

ORDINATION FOR MINISTERS' WIVES?

While the vast majority of ministers' wives neither have nor desire ministerial standing, responses suggest that those who are ordained fall into two categories. (1) There are those who have come to ministry through the vocation of their husbands, men pledged to life service for Christ and the church. Wives feel they ought to join in this action if they have the training to do so and their husbands desire it. (2) There are those who were called to ministry before they met their husband, or in a manner parallel to his call. It is *their own* vocation. In these marriages, two calls are united but do not necessarily become homogeneous.

Women in the first classification say quite frankly that they were ordained in order to be of greater assistance to their husbands. Among older women, this frequently came about when their husbands served as chaplains in the armed services. Helen Adams, aged ninety-nine, of whose ministry I have learned through her daughter,[1] took her husband's Universalist pulpit when he went into the First World War. She had had seminary training along with him and was examined before being permitted to serve his church. She expected to return to the role of minister's wife when her husband came home, but nearby churches without pastors kept asking for her help. "In some cases the churches were almost defunct, and she rebuilt or reorganized them," writes her daughter. "As soon as they were on their feet, she turned them over to another minister. There was no conflict with her marriage or the raising of her children." Events of this kind were more numerous during World War II. Women were also pressed into service during depression years.

Middle-aged and young respondents in this group, however, were frequently ordained to assist their husbands with multiple churches. One says, "I went into the ministry and chose to be ordained for the sole purpose of helping my husband in a larger parish in southern Iowa and northern Missouri. At one time we had twelve churches in the parish." She took special responsibility for education, was designated associate minister and normally preached three times each Sunday. With an M. A. degree in education, she was prepared for ordination through the conference reading program.[2]

Another woman was ordained to assist her husband when he was chaplain of a large city hospital because it was felt that female patients would talk more freely with a person of their own sex. This one-time hospital chaplain later became professor of theology in a seminary.

The question may well be raised: what happens to these women when their husbands move on into positions which no longer require their assistance as ordained persons? Do their ordination vows just evaporate?

The first woman cited above now teaches in a multi-ethnic ghetto school. She goes into the homes of her pupils and considers herself still very much in the ministry. She also serves as interim pastor when occasion demands, leads services of Holy Communion or otherwise engages in the proclamation of the word and administration of the sacraments, as needed, on Sundays. The second woman, in addition to such Sunday supply work, teaches confirmation

classes. (Her church requires that this be done by an ordained person.) She also conducts the Communion service
at women's retreats.[3]

It should be noted that the women in this classification
had the necessary educational qualifications for ordination.
William Douglas' study *Ministers' Wives* (most of whom
are not ordained) reveals that eighty-five percent of these
women regard themselves as deeply involved in their husbands' work.[4] Under the present norms for ordination, this
would not be a sufficient reason for giving them such status. Is it desirable that women graduates of seminaries who
marry ministers be given such standing?

Opinions differ. There are several reasons why a couple
may decide against the wife's ordination. The husband may
wish to protect her from professional involvement in the
church he serves. She herself may see no particular purpose
that would be served by this recognition. Her education
makes it possible for her to serve in some degree, whether
or not she is ordained. The couple are young; they want a
family; the time when she might use such status to the advantage of any church seems remote. Psychological factors,
also, may affect the decision: a husband may feel threatened if his wife has equal rank; a wife may assume ordination would place greater distance between herself and
members of the congregation. Without it, she can be a
"go-between" for husband and people, a non-professional
person but observing needs in a professional way. It is a
great experience to be ordained together, as couples can testify, but the position described above cannot be lightly dismissed. It has much to recommend it. A further consideration lies in the fact that the value of ordination itself is
questioned in some seminaries today.

On the other hand, a woman who has gone through
college and seminary *is* a professionally trained person but,
without ordination, many doors will remain closed to her.
In the earlier years of marriage, she may not find it frus-

trating to teach a Sunday School class, lead youth activities, go to women's meetings, sing in the choir, and do
other work on a volunteer basis. But when her children
are in school, she may wish to devote herself to the more
difficult tasks for which she has had special training. If
she is ordained, churches may inquire as to her availability
when certain positions are opening. Apart from ordination, her preparation may become a fragment of the past,
forgotten by all, herself included. Young couples graduating from seminary and considering the wife's future should
examine their motives at some depth. Does the husband
want the egoistic satisfaction of higher status than his wife?
Could his attitude, expressed honestly, be, "I belong to God
and my wife belongs to me"? Both parts of this statement
are true until conjoined, when a false note creeps in because two realms of discourse have been united as though
equal. Husband and wife belong to each other, but do not
both equally belong to God?

A woman, likewise, must ask herself straight questions:
why did I go to seminary? do I feel called to the ministry
or do I merely want status? No blanket recommendation
can be made. From correspondence with well over a dozen
women, just before or immediately following graduation
from widely scattered seminaries, I have the impression that
while some have good reasons for seeking or not seeking
ordination, others are under rather heavy pressure not to do
so. Perhaps the church should take a fresh look at the vocation of minister's wife. Prepared couples are commissioned
together when they go to an overseas station for mission
work. What is so different about the home field at this
stage in history?

Whereas ordination for the classification of ministers'
wives we have just been considering was a matter of personal policy and strategy when a woman had adequate education, the much larger group, now to be discussed, presents
an altogether different picture. They were called to the

ministry prior to meeting their husband or in a manner independent of his vocation. They want to help their marriage partner but feel that his work does not inexorably define theirs. Sooner or later, many women, married to ministers, recognize that they are attracted to a type of work different from that of a "typical minister's wife."

The realization, whenever it comes, can cause anxious hours during which the couple work through their feelings and expectations of one another. There may be more or less tension, depending on the extent to which either husband, wife, or both are bound to the role expectations of their families, the Christian community, or others. The problem cannot be solved independently by either husband or wife. A correspondent tells about two friends of hers, both of whom were ministers: after their marriage, the husband said, "From now on, *I* do the preaching." The wife, confined to work with the children of his parish, does not feel this is the task for which she is best fitted. Has her spouse been highhanded?

On the other side, it is just as unfair for a woman, after marriage, to take the attitude, "I am a minister, *not* a minister's wife," dismissing all responsibility for her husband's work. No one can make exclusively personal decisions, affecting both parties in marriage, and expect happiness. The minister who takes a wife (or a husband) can no longer think wholly in terms of "my work"; he or she is now answerable for the development of an additional vocation, that of the partner. As I have said, it is difficult to work through to the right solution, but it is not impossible. If a man and woman have married deep in the love of one another and of God, both vocations will grow in a way which is mutually enriching and a blessing to the world.

Concrete examples will make this clearer. A young woman, ordained in the Baptist Church, married a Presbyterian minister. Her own church took the attitude that she should settle down to be a "good minister's wife." She, nev-

ertheless, impelled toward a specialized ministry which required further education, is now serving as assistant minister in a church which does not itself ordain women, and is
continuing her education with the full cooperation of her
husband. The church of which he is pastor is also sympathetic and has done everything possible to make their home
duties light. The church she is serving, together with its senior pastor, accepts her as she is. Older clergy ask, "Is your
husband taking courses too? Isn't he threatened by what
you are doing?" Fortunately, she knows he is not. The couple appear to understand one another; their days off coin-
cide; they do housework together. There are, at present,
no children. A number of younger respondents wish to
complete graduate studies before beginning their families.
Others are pursuing graduate studies and alternate in the
care of the children, or have made other arrangements for
their care.

Flora Slosson, a young pastor in the United Church of
Christ, married Wilhelm Wuellner, a Lutheran minister.
Instead of continuing to serve a church on her own, she became involved in small group ministry in a large church of
her denomination. This has made it easier for her to be at
home during the preschool years of their three children.
Work with Bible study and prayer groups has also led to
the writing of her first book, *Prayer and the Living
Christ*.[5] Her husband is a seminary professor; she occasionally teaches a course, too. Mrs. Wuellner says:

> An unmarried woman can give more time to her ministry,
> but perhaps a married woman can give more understanding
> because of her own experience of family life. In my case
> I find that things I have learned through marriage and
> motherhood have given me outlooks which make me a
> better person—and thus a better minister in the long run.

She has exchanged a wooden pulpit for a paper pulpit. Has
she left the ministry or ceased proclaiming the word?

Even when persons of the same denomination marry, their calling may develop in different ways. Sometimes it is the husband who specializes while the wife is a pastor. He may be a hospital chaplain, a teacher, or pastor of one church, while his wife ministers to another. A young woman was licensed to preach during seminary days in order to help her husband with a charge [6] while he was going to school. Later, a congregation "asked the bishop and cabinet if I might not be appointed to serve them." She answered this call, returned to seminary and was ordained. She and her husband have continued to serve as pastors of different churches of the same denomination.

How does she manage?

> We just share and share alike—no chiefs and all Indians in our home. We have no "man" and "woman" duties, and our churches have priority on our time. Our only daughter is married but she was not when I went into the ministry. She loved our life, and so she married a Methodist minister also.

A vocation to specialized ministry may appear even further along in the life of a woman married to a minister. The thought of ordination had never crossed Dorothy Faust's mind. For fifteen years she had been director of reconciliation in the Court of Domestic Relations in Columbus, Ohio. During part of that time, she had been a director of Christian education, since that had been her undergraduate major. She also did marriage counseling with her husband, pastor of a Christian (Disciples of Christ) Church in Columbus.

Mrs. Faust left court work, graduated from law school, and then studied with the Council for Clinical Training to improve her counseling skills. It came as a surprise when three of her chaplain supervisors in hospitals recommended to the examining board of her denomination that she be ordained; they thought she should remain in chaplaincy work. She was ordained in 1957, took advanced clinical training, and was accredited by the Council for Clinical Training as a chaplain supervisor. Her work had been done in correctional, special, mental, and general hospitals. Accredited also by the American Protestant Hospital Association, she went to Grant Hospital in Columbus under the advisement of the Ohio Council of Churches. She is now a full-time chaplain supervisor, recognized as the head of a department and paid by the hospital.[7]

The question may be raised as to the attitude of churches toward the pastor's wife who follows a ministry of her own. There is probably wide difference of opinion among parishioners. One young woman says that the first church her husband served created difficulty by objecting to her being pastor of another congregation. They felt she should be giving the benefits of her education to their own church school. In the past, many churches have realized their hope of receiving two ministers for the price of one, but times are changing. The possibility of two persons giving the major portion of their time on one salary is diminishing. A woman cannot usually give even half of her time to a church and adequately care for her own family without help. Children in the parsonage home must be educated and the cost of education is climbing faster than most ministerial salaries. While not expecting their wives to work, husbands, nevertheless, may appreciate their willingness to do so. A woman whose interest centers in the church may prefer to follow a church vocation at a lower salary than she could command in another position which would allow her to be with her husband on Sunday. This is a family matter. It is difficult to see the basis on which a congregation could object if it is paying only one minister's salary. Many church members doubtless recognize that pastors' wives are just as human as their own daughters and accept their desire to reach a family decision as to where they can be most useful.

ORDAINED WIVES OF LAYMEN

Fifty-eight respondents are ministers' wives, many of whom have an additional ministry. Fifty-one are wives of laymen. Who are these men and where does the wife of a layman get the notion that she wants to be a minister?

The men are in the following occupations:

Wives	Occupation of husbands
17	Business (self-employed, in management positions, in labor force, and undesignated)
10	College professors and other teachers, not including seminary professors who are ordained and classed with ministers
5	Government-related employment
4	Farmers
3	Physicians
3	Engineers (chemical, civil, electrical)
3	Professions related to the arts
2	Attorneys
2	Students
1	Forester
1	Retired general of European army

As to motivation, the following incidents will show how a woman in her middle thirties, wife of a businessman, was led toward a career in the church. The young couple had been active in religious work all their lives; afterward they shared marriage, in Christian social action and various church projects. When their two children were in school, the wife began to face empty hours. What should she do with them? She decided that she wanted to become a minister of education. Already a college graduate, she began seminary studies, which posed no problem as there was a seminary in their city. Her husband was in full accord with her desire. He had earlier been through a crisis in his own vocation and had gone into business for himself, so he understood her restlessness to be using her time in a worthwhile way. Her fourth-grade son thought, "Mother must be stupid to have to go back to school now" but changed his mind when he saw her grades. She did her field work in a small church within driving distance of their home.

She sought ordination after graduation from seminary; however, the association [8] in which her home church was located said "no" because it did not want to ordain a person to part-time service, and the church in which she was working was in another association. This decision was made despite the fact that clergy and deacons of her very large home church had recommended her unanimously. Her children were now in their teens. She asked why ministers' wives could be ordained when some of them, apparently, were not holding positions separate from their husbands' work, and was told this was a "courtesy." (The assumption underlying the practice is that a professionally trained minister's wife will have ample opportunity to give herself to ministry, and the status is seldom denied her if the couple ask.) The situation of the layman's wife seems more ambiguous. It should be kept in mind that clergy opinion still dominates most association meetings.

The individual under discussion did not accept defeat over the refusal of ordination by one association but appealed to the association in which the church she served was located. Her request was granted and ordination followed. With her children becoming more self-sufficient, she has now gone into full-time service as an assistant minister in a city church not far from her home. While her special responsibility is education, according to her own choice, she is free to engage in pastoral work to the limit of her ability.

In writing to the Romans, the apostle Paul said, "The

gifts and the call of God are irrevocable." [9] I do not want to make a big point of this with regard to the call of women for three reasons: (1) the apostle was talking about a whole people and not individuals; the relationship between "universal" and "particular" would have to be discussed; (2) proof texts are outmoded; and (3) the doctrine of election has always caused controversy among theologians and could not be discussed briefly. But a case like the one to be described next, which is not isolated, does bring Paul's words to mind.

A woman who is now the wife of a forester had been called to the ministry as a young girl but felt insecure in her motivation. Was it because her church did not ordain women? When she married, she joined her husband in the United Church of Christ. Ministers were needed in the area where they were to make their home. Events began to push her: "the need, the call, the fact that I had the ability; study, prayer, counseling." Finally, she said, "If anyone wants to use me as a minister, I'll try it." Her theological training was obtained through a conference study program with courses in a lay school of theology conducted by an Eastern seminary. She is now the sole pastor of a "larger parish" [10] made up of three small churches which, together, can barely afford one staff person. Her husband, a loyal churchman, cooperates fully with her work, often attends all three churches with her, and sings in the choir. He is a deacon in one of the churches; the people have great respect for him. "The children don't seem to mind being p. k.'s [preacher's kids] and often give me advice," she says. "All my mental turbulence settled down when I became willing to enter the ministry and I was able to meet the real turbulence of working in the church of Jesus Christ with his people."

Another pastor, wife of a salesman and mother of two children, has followed a path similar to the one just described. She left the church in which she grew up (one that does not ordain women) to join her husband, who was a Methodist. In time, she became district spiritual-life secretary for the Women's Society of Christian Service. Then, they moved. Going to the church nearest them, they found it was without minister or money. The district superintendent "asked if I would preach a few weeks to see if any interest could be generated. It was. The church began to grow. I was asked to stay on as pastor." After discussing the matter with her husband and church authorities, she agreed to serve until conference time, four or five months away. She took preliminary steps toward licensure for preaching. All of this happened while she was otherwise employed and subsequent illness forced her to make a decision about her future work. With the concurrence of her family, she chose the church. The road to ordination took hard work and much study, but she followed it gladly. One can understand why she says, "I don't feel that I chose the ministry; I sincerely believe that God placed me into it, knocked down the many barriers before me, and has kept me there." A realist, she thinks there will always be opposition to women in the professions. The "image" carried in the minds of many pastoral relations committees, she says, is that a minister is "a white male about thirty-five years old."

A male minister had warned her early that there would be a certain amount of jealousy on the part of men because they resent woman's equality, and on the part of women because she was young and did not fit the image some have of women ministers: "large framed, bosomy, hair pulled back, masculine, bossy." In fact, however, she has been encouraged by the number of women who said "they could confide their personal problems better to me because I was a woman." She also has many friends among male clergy and feels accepted by them in her work.

The wife of a university professor entered the ministry by quite a different route, one which only a few respon-

4-7371

dents have taken. Fascinated by languages in college, she decided to interrupt her course to study Greek and Hebrew at a seminary near her home. She enjoyed this so much that she finished and was graduated cum laude, but without a degree.[11] Then, completing her college work, she went on to acquire an M. A. in English, after which she preached for the then Congregational Church for some time before joining and being ordained. "Since I had a real sense of mission," she remarks, "I did not mind taking a small church and working at making it into a strong one. This has been my pleasure several times." When she married, her husband was in total sympathy with her pastoral work and has remained so.

Seminary colleagues might have predicted that he would dine on Hebrew nouns and Greek verbs but no such disaster lay before him. This respondent loves homemaking: "I resent women looking down on womanly duties as second-rate activities—keeping a home is an exciting thing. I have one real plus in my life, and that is a husband who also loves his home, does not resent the chores involved, and appreciates the open doors and hospitality we have maintained. I am sure the key to it all is the right man."

WHAT DO HUSBANDS THINK?

Since I have not corresponded with husbands, this section is written as a summary of my respondents' assessments of male outlook, a risky business. No direct questions on this matter were put to the women and information as to the attitude of the spouse was given voluntarily.

Two points have become clear through this study, however. First, married women ministers seem quite happy. Without exception, they indicate that a woman's ministry is enriched by marriage, even though the actual hours spent in serving the church are fewer than single women can give. It seems doubtful to me that women could be experiencing gratification in their work if husbands were unhappy or withdrawn. Male clergy are well aware of the extent to which the atmosphere of their homes affects their work. Perhaps nothing so handicaps any minister, man or woman, as the feeling that he or she is failing to further the happiness of those who are nearest. In general, my respondents reflect a favorable home environment.

A second point seems equally clear. This environment has not been created by the wave of a magic wand. Husband and wife have made a real effort to understand one another and to adjust to one another in accordance with a Christian view of life. Only two respondents, apart from the divorced eleven, married men who were not in full sympathy with their work. One, a widow, writes, "My husband said I married the church instead of him, but he later came to love the church as I did. His remark was, 'You lived your message.'"

The other, a young woman, married a man who grew up in a conservative denomination which he had rejected because he could not reconcile its teaching with studies done for a career in science. While still in college, he told my respondent that he wanted to marry a professional woman. This was prior to her clear decision to become a minister. He said he felt such a wife would make a much more interesting long-term companion. Before their marriage, he accepted with some reluctance her desire to enter the ministry but his hostility toward the church remained. He has, however, been supportive of her decision.

The husbands of two other correspondents went through illnesses of such critical nature, early in the marriage, that the wife had to become breadwinner for the family. In both instances the husbands, though invalids, have done everything possible to further the wife's ministry. One of these women had done significant work with youth prior to her marriage, with fifteen young men deciding to become ministers largely as a result of her leadership. She supports the family by teaching but is also pastor of two small churches in an area where a number of congregations are without ministerial service.

With the exceptions already noted, husbands are devoted members of the church. Many of them hold offices in the congregations served by their wives, acting on a board, teaching in church school, leading a scout troop, participating in the choir, or otherwise fitting in where needed. A husband who is doing graduate work in English leads a reading group which is tracing religious themes in modern literature. Women married to businessmen say that they draw on their husbands' knowledge for church administration. If these men were the milquetoast type, it seems improbable that they could succeed so well in meeting their own occupational demands.

Respondent after respondent heaped praises upon husbands. One says, "My husband is special. He is a man in his own profession and is not threatened by me. He has great regard for my integrity and position. He has patience and willingness to share me with others." This man, like many others, helps his wife when she is under special pressure and she does the same with him. Another says, "I am sure that men like my husband are hard to find, but I would not have married unless I had found such a person. I have known women trained for the ministry who married and virtually left it. I could not have done this." [12] A minister's wife says they can take each other's place in either home or church work. Others claim their husbands want them to use their gifts and training, and encourage them to do all they can.

Perhaps my respondents are perceptive enough to be aware of the deep needs of their spouses and children and to govern the work they undertake and their methods of doing it with this in mind. One of the most difficult problems they meet is moving. A pastor, the wife of a farmer who also has a paper-hanging and painting business, was asked by her conference minister to undertake larger parish work which required strong ecumenical commitment. Her long ministry in one church had been successful but it was time for a change. This woman had looked toward the ministry from early adolescence. She had known that marriage would be precluded for her "if God did not see fit to provide the right mate." She also believes, though, that a husband should be the head of the household. Her mate earns the major part of the family living and much of her salary goes into the church. They thought about the move for a year before attempting it, viewing what it would mean to each of them from every angle. It seems to have turned out well.

In some cases, husbands and wives independently explore possibilities for future service before deciding on a move. They then go where each will have maximum opportunity. This may delay decision a year or so but they feel it is worth the delay. The majority of married women ministers think the husband's employment must be considered first because he is responsible, in the eyes of society, for the support of his family. This does not disturb them for, as one says, "I have never had any trouble finding worthwhile work to do." None of these women deny that there have been problems, but all affirm that they have been able to meet them and can understand the lives of others better because of them.

Possibly most men would find it hard to analyze their feelings relative to the ordination of their wives. Each of us has a measure of selfishness with which to contend. A good minister, man or woman, cherishes family relationships, but whoever marries a minister marries a person in whose life God has priority. Something in the partner has given genuine response to the quality of this commitment, or else the marriage would not have taken place. A common ground exists upon which they can build but, undoubtedly, there are times of ambivalence and ambiguity with regard to the wife's profession on the part of both. We do not escape our humanity, but it is easy to sense a lasting love in the quality of marital relationship revealed, perhaps unconsciously, by most of my respondents.

DIVORCE

As has been mentioned, eleven respondents are divorced. In several instances, the divorce took place before the woman had even contemplated being a minister. It is impossible to know whether a beginning sense of call on the part of the wife could have figured in the man's wish to be free. In at least three cases, and possibly in four or five, the husband's departure seems to have been precipitated by the wife's ministry. One professional man who fully understood his wife's commitment before marriage found that it was too much for him to accept afterwards. A husband who had encouraged his wife to prepare for the ministry later deserted her for a younger person. Another husband was advised by his psychiatrist to dissolve the relationship as a health measure for himself. These men were obviously disturbed to the point of crisis by the wife's professional status and what it did to their lives. In the few remaining cases, there was a radical difference in values which may not have been apparent to the couple prior to or even in the early days of marriage, but which became more than either could endure as time went on. They were simply going different ways and a pretense of marital unity was impossible. These divorced women are continuing in varied forms of ministry and make a significant contribution to the church.

Do Married Women Ministers Want Children?

The evidence points to the fact that women ministers want to be mothers. Respondents average slightly more than two children to a couple. Twelve indicated they had children but did not say how many; five married late in life. Aside from these women, the statistics are:

Women	Children per family	Total
16	0	0
12	1	12
31	2	62
18	3	54
12	4	48
3	7	21

There are several factors to be taken into consideration here. Seven of the childless women are young and several specifically state that they want to have a family. Others in the childless group may represent late marriages which did not appear as such in the response. A more accurate estimate could have been made if the date of marriage had been ascertained and compared with the age grouping and date of ordination. Young couples who may want more than one or two children may also complicate any statistical analysis.

No married respondent indicated that she preferred to remain childless. Several who have no children or only one child imply a medical limitation. One young woman, asked whether or not she thought childlessness might be desirable for professional couples, replied that she and her husband had "certainly thought of the possibility." They concluded, however, that a decision not to have children in order to further their joint service to society would be immature and show a lack of faith in the future:

I am frankly suspicious of anyone who talks like this. Most of the people I know are compulsive workers and "escape artists." It is too easy to identify "service to society" with "my career," and without children it's even easier—there is not the slightest brake on SELF.

She is convinced that a couple who can't "make it" with a home and family has no reason to expect society to take their ministry seriously. This couple has two children.

A mother of one child (who had miscarried four) said they had helped to raise and educate nine. Upon further inquiry, she offered this explanation:

First, let me say that all of them came from rural districts out of reach of bus service but were eager for an education. We not only had them as members of the household but tried to see that each had some responsibility about the place, ample time to study, whatever recreation the school sponsored and whatever time they needed for taking part in sports.

The children spent from three to more than five years with this couple. Two went into the ministry. The couple are loved as grandparents by the children of those who lived in their home.

This is, of course, not a typical case, as few of my respondents live in so isolated an area, but many express the desire to keep an open house for children and youth and to do everything possible to be of help to them. Several offer foster care.

THE ATTITUDE OF CHILDREN

Who can determine the attitude of a child toward his parents' work? It is changeable and related to his own concerns of the moment. That children are impressed by a view of their mother acting in an entirely different setting, the church, is evidenced by two little boys whose first exposure to public worship took place about the same time they were taken to visit a zoo: "Lord, have mercy hippot'mus" was chanted around the house the next day. In another instance, a mother of four says her brood play church on Sunday evening.

One is acolyte, one minister, one lector and one the choir. The dolls are the congregation. They have no preference as to who is minister as they have heard both men and women. The only requirement is that the lector must know how to read. The minister wears a bathrobe; the offering plate is usually full of buttons, but what always interests us most is the sermon, a rehash of what was heard that morning in church. We are seldom invited to the "service," so what we hear is spontaneous and uninhibited.

Children work out their own little philosophies about the work of parents. A Baptist minister's wife, mother of three, was called to be pastor of a church to which she was giving interim service about the same time her husband was asked to take a position in denominational fund raising which required a great deal of travel. Their children were in school. When the youngest was asked by his teacher about the parents' occupation, he had it all figured out: "My father is a preacher of funds; my mother is a preacher of the Gospel."

A child may be proud of the respect shown his minister-mother but, at the same time, dislike sharing her with other people. One mother sees this necessity of sharing her as a valuable experience for her children, but poignant remarks may be heard that make her weigh her responsibilities carefully. One little boy who did not want his mother to leave him in the evening said, "Mommy, you stay up all night with someone who is sick or going to die. What would you do if I got sick?" "That cut me to bits," wrote the minister-mother who has to work to support her children. In this instance, the children have the care of older members of the family.

There are encouraging remarks too: "Our older daughter said recently, 'I want to be a minister like you when I grow up,'" but, in contrast, another mother heard, "I hate people. They're always taking my Mommy away from me." There is, however, a sequel to this story. When the daughter was in college, her mother was under fire for commending the school board for opening the schools to black students. She received "hate" letters and telephone calls.

> Our daughter did a right-about-face on the segregation issue while listening to such statements as "I hope they rape your daughter." As one caller asked for enlightenment as to what a Christian's attitude ought to be, we were astounded to hear her answering from our integration point of view. When asked about it, she said, "Well, he really seemed to want an answer, and when I began to express my thoughts, I realized you were right."

In an M. A. thesis, "The Leadership of Women in the Christian Church," Miss Elaine Marsh includes a letter from the ordained minister-mother of Dr. Howard Stone Anderson, pastor of the First Congregational Church in Washington, D. C. Mrs. Anderson wrote that when her only son was married,

> his bride was a university and seminary trained young woman and he wished her to be ordained at the same time he was. That took place in my St. Louis Church. I have always felt it was one of the highest compliments I ever received, as a mother and as a preacher, that my son wished his wife to be ordained. I felt as though I had not failed in my motherly duties because I was doing church work.

Of his mother's ministry, Dr. Anderson s s, "My great recollection was of a very creative, original mind. Consequently her sermons were fresh, vivid, interesting and inspirational, as well as helpful."

My study reveals that quite a number of children from families where both parents are ministers themselves go into the service of the church. Many also go into professions that call for counseling or otherwise helping human beings. A girl, whose ordained mother hoped she would choose a church vocation for which she was well qualified, said, "Not on your life! You can't have special friends in the ministry and I couldn't stand that." [13] But after one year of grade-school teaching, she was chosen to represent her part of the country as the "Outstanding Teacher of the Disadvantaged." She also gave time to a leadership education program in which churches of her city were cooperating. Another woman minister, whose children didn't like the "gold-fish bowl existence" when they were younger, says that they have since told her how much they learned from the many kinds of people coming into the parsonage. A concern for others, to which children growing up in parsonage homes are habitually exposed, carries over into other vocations as well as the ministry. Although they may pass through periods of rebellion, most such children become strong church members in adult life, if not earlier.

But children also help their parents. One mother says they gave her a deeper understanding of other young people in the parish; she found it much easier to relate to the various age groups represented by her own children. Youngsters run in and out of the minister's home in quite a different way when their friends are members of the manse family. "Our boys are four and seven," a new pastor told his congregation the first Sunday. "We'll have no secrets from you folks." An ordained mother, visiting her daughter (now mother of four) in a distant state, tells of their reminiscences:

Many of my daughter's happiest memories were directly or indirectly the result of the fact that "Mamma was a minister," and the whole family stood with her. There were some inconveniences, to be sure, but the advantages and blessings outweigh them from this standpoint.

CAN A WOMAN MANAGE TWO CAREERS?

When a woman tries to be both homemaker and pastor, she may face conflicting demands upon her time. Which has priority—home or church? A number point out that this is the same problem any working woman has to meet. Respondents express three points of view. One group says, "The church comes first." They do not neglect their families. They hire some domestic help, household tasks are divided, prepared foods are frequently used; they make a sharp distinction between housekeeping and homemaking and are usually well organized. Says one, "It's not a matter of insufficient time so much as planning and deciding most important priorities. As there's no future in housework, I neglected all but the most essential and learned quick methods for that." A second group would argue, "The home comes first." As one respondent expresses it:

Keeping a home is the first responsibility. Time may be an element. I have used limited funds to hire help at particular times. Children's studies, school trips, etc. all have to be worked into a schedule with proper perspective.

Perhaps if one were to talk at length with those expressing the above viewpoints, it would be discovered that their position does not differ so very much from the largest third group which finds it impossible to assign priority to either home or church. Both are parts of the ministry of an ordained married woman. They think that they can distinguish, with the help of God, where their presence is most essential at any given moment. As one extremely busy pastor puts it, "I'm afraid that I just live as the day demands. My home, profession and study are so intertwined I would find it almost impossible to divide them. My whole self is involved." Another woman remarked during an interview that she does not find any special tension between her home and church duties: "You just use the time you have to much better advantage and members of the family pitch in and do their share."

My own observation has been that employed women in general seem quite attentive to the needs of their children. Unemployed women often spend hours away from their homes in volunteer work and social activities which may be more in line with the traditional role of homemaker but do not in themselves insure a better family relationship. In an article, "Effects of Maternal Employment on Children," assessing results of research, Lois Meek Stolz of the Stanford University department of psychology says, "It looks as if the fact of the mother being employed or staying at home is not such an important factor in determining the behavior of the child as we have been led to think." [14] A respondent writes, "My son is a rebel and has had a difficult time growing up. More than one psychiatrist has been surprised to learn that having a ministerial mother hasn't been a factor in his disturbance." As much as fifteen years ago, I heard a school psychologist make the statement that at least sixty percent of the influences beating upon children come from outside their homes. Perhaps today his estimate would be even higher. Many women try to improve the lot of children by working in vocations that affect a broader segment of youthful society than could ever be reached from their individual dwellings, and some young mothers, with great love of children, have found a vocation of their own in caring for those of others. Public child care centers do not seem to be the only alternative to the home.

The working mother provides a convenient scapegoat

for the ills of society. Perhaps a socially induced sense of guilt makes her feel doubly responsible for her children's behavior, but the notion that all would be well if women would stay in their homes is simplistic. There seems little doubt that, in the United States, at least, some children have had too much mothering and too little fathering. As women lend a hand in the support of the family, men may be able, in time, to see more of their children. A period of rapid transition is difficult for everyone but as Gregory Baum, commenting on secular emphasis in theology, says, "It is in this coming-to-be of the human world that God's Word is present." [15]

From time to time, I have spoken of divine call and professional competence as though they were interchangeable phrases. This may not be acceptable to everyone. The question recurs in one form or another: does God call women or do they, wanting to be useful, choose professional ministry on their own initiative? Perhaps it is not necessary to polarize the question in this way, for does not the life history of each person unfold with reference to God and to human beings? The phrases would then be two sides of the same coin.

A woman, like a man, may hear the divine call as she ponders changing circumstances of her own existence, as she tries to understand what she really wants from life, where she is going. Like a man, she, too, may become aware of an inner voice speaking to her. There are experiences which cannot be accounted for by psychology, sociology or even theology. They come from "out there" or "in there," from a source so high or deep that the origin seems inaccessible. If we say they come from God, this does not mean that we can give a scientific account of what we mean by "God," much less explicate his purpose. The right road may be determined through following the clearest intimation of truth we have.

When a woman is married, her choices are made with

due reference to husband and children. (The same is true for a man.) She weighs their views carefully; growing Christian experience and prayer clarify her inner vision. But strong impulses, even in a person who prays with sincerity, may have complex derivation. They cannot be followed blindly. One may need psychiatric help if the departure from social norms is too pronounced, but God is never in a hurry. Integrity is met by integrity. If a married woman is being called by him, she will have more than subjective states to reassure her. Others will sense her call. A path will open if she desires to be receptive to any indication of the divine will in the ordering of events. Only dishonesty or cowardice can permanently block God's purpose in any life.

The fullness of God's will, however, also requires the responsiveness of the Christian community. If we consider subjective states alone, perhaps the call of men and women differs little. If this is true, then in God's spirit we should be able to understand one another. Indeed this may even be the chief locale for profound understanding of ministry across the dividing line of sex.

5.

The Ministry of Widows

"Come quick, Mrs. Duke! One of my old ladies is dying and I can't get a soul to sit with her. Won't you come over and say a prayer for her right away?" Turning off her washing machine, the minister's wife left with her next-door neighbor, who was matron of a home for the aging and elderly poor.

"I found the woman lying on a narrow cot bed," recalls Mrs. Duke, who was widowed some years after this incident took place. "She was very frail and very fearful. Sitting down by her side, I repeated the twenty-third Psalm, praying with her and for her. Before leaving that room, I resolved that I would one day become a minister of the Gospel for the help of the elderly."

Following the death of her husband, she served as lay minister of a church while attending seminary (she had previously graduated from Simmons College School of Social Work). Her intern year was spent at Havenwood Retirement Community in Concord, New Hampshire. She received her divinity degree and was recently ordained to the ministry.

Mrs. Duke is one of forty-six respondents who have been widowed: thirty-five by the death of their husbands and eleven through divorce. They have in common the experience of marriage with all it has brought of happiness or grief; they do not face the problem of balancing the needs of a husband against those of a profession. Their lives are so diverse that they share little else except faith in God.

AN UNSOUGHT MINISTRY

Many of these widows would not have undertaken professional work voluntarily. The older ones, especially, would have considered a career beyond homemaking more than they could handle. For example, Hilda Ives, octogenarian and recipient of four honorary degrees, would have laughed at anyone suggesting she might become a minister. Her life as wife of a promising young lawyer was full and happy. At first, the couple had been only nominal church members but later reached the decision to take a more active part for the sake of their children who, they knew, needed Christian education and would be unlikely to respond to it if their parents remained aloof.

Then, suddenly, Mr. Ives caught influenza and died in less than two weeks, leaving his thirty-year-old widow with five children. "It seemed as though I had been pitched over a precipice," she wrote; intellectual problems, practical problems, the sheer horror of emptiness and aloneness shut out all help. Her pastor wisely steered her toward the Gospels. She writes:

> One night in great suffering, I cried out into the darkness of my room, "God of Heaven, help me. I can't help

myself." Instantly I seemed to be held by a pervading strength and peace. Tears stopped. For some hours, in a way that words cannot explain, I knew the incoming of a life not my own. That was the beginning of my knowledge that heartfelt prayer brings the reality and resources of a living God.

Remembering that experience, she continues:

> To a person of faith the death of a loved one is an agony, sustained by the living comfort of God. To a person who has not found God a real presence, available, sustaining and comforting, death of a loved one is sheer despair.[1]

An admirer of those who had spiritual strength and dedication, she once dropped the half-facetious remark to a home missionary of her acquaintance that she wished he could make a missionary of her.

Mrs. Ives went to work for Baby Hygiene and Child Welfare in Portland, Maine, where she became instrumental in establishing the first day nursery and the first open-air school for children with tubercular tendencies. She initiated the first pure milk station in Portland, for which the city later took responsibility. Always she tried to find visual ways of presenting problems to the citizens. When a "swat the fly" campaign was under way, she secured the cooperation of a pharmacist who agreed to pay a penny to each child who brought in one hundred dead flies. The flies were put into a window lined with posters showing the insects hovering over food with highly visible germs clinging to their legs. Hordes of small customers, selling flies and buying candy, jammed the store. The window became an impressive sight, but adult customers could scarcely reach a counter; although the project soon had to be abandoned, the city had gotten the point.

The same resourcefulness led to better care for babies. She planned tableaux for a men's service club luncheon at which she had been invited to speak. "We worked for contrast between needs that were being met and those that were not," Mrs. Ives explained. One tableau showed a live syphilitic baby in a crib. Four sets of twins from different ethnic backgrounds were featured in another. "As a climax we had the prettiest nurse we could find, holding a beautiful healthy baby in her arms; she looked like a madonna." The young widow's speech boasted twelve words. "Gentlemen," she said, pointing to the baby, "if you give us money, this is what we can do." Money poured in and the visual projection did not have to be repeated the following year.

Mrs. Ives had forgotten her remark to the missionary but he had not. One day he asked her to begin work in an island church. "Let me think about it," she gasped. "I never imagined you would take me seriously—but I do want to be of use to God in this world. Let me call you in a few days." Her answer was, "No." She had to think about her children and dismissed all consideration of the call.

A year passed and the missionary tried again. "I have just the place for you this summer—a lovely little town with doctors nearby for your offspring. It's also a healthful climate. A little church needs your leadership, sixty-two miles away in the hills." She agreed, half afraid, but the church said in no uncertain terms that it would not have a woman. "You must go just the same," the missionary declared, in reply to her protest. The conference paid most of the cost and the church could not make an independent decision.

"Go just the same with a unanimous vote against me?" She was incredulous.

"Go just the same," was the calm reply.

Upon arrival at the church, the deacon greeted her sincerely but with resignation, "Ain't no use your coming here," he said. "This place is dead, just as dead as it can be. Every one they send is wuss than the one before and the last one is always the wust of all."[2] He meant no offense and she was sympathetic. Investigating, she learned that, for sixty years, the little church had had old ministers, sick ministers, or young theological students. Now, a woman!

Mrs. Ives brought the same imagination to the ministry that she had given to social work in Portland. Her people were desperately poor. She took their produce and flowers to the city when she drove in the first of each week and brought back the money. A carload of friends drove up to her parish one Sunday morning for church. Following the service a deacon brought her a ten-dollar bill. "There's been a terrible mistake," he said. "Somebody meant to put in a dollar and put in ten." That was all right, she answered.

In relating the story, her eyes danced. "He looked at me as though I were a pagan—refusing to return money that did not belong to the church." She assured him that city people had more money coming in, could afford to give and should do so. Still doubtful, he accepted her judgment.

At first, a pillar of the church was showered with dire predictions as to the results of her pastorate by a fellow farmer and non-church member. The "pillar" defended her, saying, "You're all wrong about that woman. I heard her talk the other night and the folks liked her real well. I'll bet you five dollars now that there'll be thirty people in that church before the summer's over—not twelve."

"Five it is," was the quick reply.

The congregation exuded satisfaction as this unchurched man appeared each Sunday, never suspecting that he had come to count heads. The seventh week, the influx of her friends brought attendance to thirty-four. That was when she learned the truth. Her defender, a winner, said heartily, "I told Jones seven weeks ago on the rud that where the carcass is, there the folks will gather." [3]

Mrs. Ives, concerned about competition among small churches of different denominations, none of which could afford a minister, tried to form larger parishes and bring about church unity. After twelve years in this work and the founding of four such parishes, she was called to be rural secretary of the Massachusetts Federation of Churches; later, serving on the faculty of Andover Newton Theological Seminary, she supervised men in rural churches, preaching all over the state herself. She assisted in the ordination of her younger son to the ministry; three of her grandsons are preparing for ordination. She still gives interim service to churches on occasion and is active in the suicide prevention program.

A PROPHETIC WORD

Hilda Ives was among the persons who contributed to Margaret Henrichsen's decision to enter the ministry. The latter, a Sunday School teacher of ten-year-olds in suburban Boston, was attending a meeting in her own church. Noting the large number of gifted leaders in the group and aware of the stark deprivation of other communities not far away, she rebelled against the blindness which, while providing the finest Christian education for members of church, neglects the spiritual needs of disadvantaged children. After the meeting, she went home and expressed herself vigorously to her husband, who consoled her with the words, "Perhaps some day you can do something about it." [4]

When, in the devastating loneliness following her husband's death, she was groping toward a plan for her life, Hilda Ives suggested the ministry. At first Mrs. Henrichsen was amused at the idea: she must find work immediately; how could she afford a seminary education? Who would want to hear a woman preach, anyhow? But that very night she wrote a former pastor to ask whether he thought there might be a closed church where a woman minister could prove acceptable. He called her on the phone with his answer. Two months from the day Hilda Ives spoke to her, she started for Maine.

Mrs. Henrichsen had had experience in both teaching

and social work; she now had to make her in-service theological preparation through a conference reading course. This required the mastering of twelve books a year. Papers had to be written endlessly, for almost every chapter of every book had its assigned written work. On six books a year examinations were given—and these six books were naturally the harder, heavier and more important ones.[5] In her study of homiletics, some of the assignments of sermon subjects were good; others disgusted or amused her. "The prize," she reports, "was to outline and write out in full a talk which you would make to the men of your church at some informal meeting on 'The Common Faults and Noble Virtues of Men.' " The heroes of this sermon were to be the biblical characters Joab, Abner and David. She thought the men of her congregation knew their faults all too well and, as for their noble virtues, "I would have been under suspicion as a scheming woman." In addition to private study, for several years she spent her vacation periods at Union Theological Seminary in New York City. As a result of this training, she saw the need for continuing study of the entire Bible and developed a habit of disciplined work. She reached the firm conviction that, important as the "know how" books are to the minister, far more significant is the "know Who," so that Christian faith and experience grow into "a deep friendship, a love affair between a man and Christ." [6]

Under Mrs. Henrichsen's leadership, a parish of two churches grew to seven. On Sunday morning and afternoon, one service followed another as quickly as she could drive from place to place. She says that she had never expected to have a higher moment on earth than her marriage, but when the day of her ordination came, it brought a still higher happiness. She had felt all along that her ministry, which began on the anniversary of her husband's birthday, met with his approval, and that he was sharing her adventure.

Mrs. Henrichsen is now a district superintendent of the United Methodist Church in Maine.

WIDOWS IN DENOMINATIONAL WORK

Several other widowed respondents are engaged in denominational work. Keeping in mind the nuances of the word "call," it is surprising to notice how often their attraction to the ministry began early in life. Guidance counselors say that seeds of a career are frequently planted in the preadolescent period and that a self-concept begins to form in adolescence. This was the case with a Unitarian-Universalist widow whose father had insisted that education was the only work suitable for a girl wanting to major in religion. She deferred to his judgment to the extent of getting her master of arts degree with a major in religious education, but took as many courses as she could from the school of theology. Her undergraduate electives had also been chosen with the ultimate goal of the ordained ministry in mind. Because graduate degrees in divinity were not approved for women at the time, she did her doctoral work in psychology. Writing many years later, she says,

> I have followed a somewhat checkered course, having gone back and forth from the church world to the academic world on a number of occasions, partly depending on what was available (since I think a married woman does go where her husband goes), and partly on interests. I have been a director of religious education, a general minister, and for two years held two churches jointly with my husband (we each preached alternate months in each of the churches). For the past twelve years, and part time before that, I have been serving at denominational headquarters in a variety of capacities.

She is now engaged in editorial work.

Wide practical experience is fully as important in denominational work as academic preparation. A Disciples of Christ woman who had wanted, even as a child, to be a missionary, but whose parents did not encourage this desire, "even though they were good and faithful church people," became a widow while her children were in the lower grades. She had had both business and nurses' training and was able to support them, but, as they approached adult life, she became an officer in Christian Women's Fellowship, later being called as state director. "I felt that now I could have fulfillment of my lifetime dream since my family were self-supporting." Six years later, her theological education adequate, she was ordained with local, state and national leaders of her denomination participating.

Widows are often past middle age before they can give themselves fully to public ministry. One United Church of Christ widow, educated and ordained with her husband, worked so closely with him that an onlooker might have said she had forgotten all about any special work of her own and had been completely absorbed into his life. He served large churches and carried heavy denominational responsibility that made it virtually impossible for her to commit her time beyond his needs and those of their four children. She writes:

> The demands of ministry cannot be circumscribed into so many hours each day—or even night. At least I am sure that I would have found such a tension impossible to resolve or even to handle. It was hard enough at times when the children were young to accept the demands upon my husband's time.

Together they participated in the ordination of their oldest son; her husband preached the sermon and she offered the ordaining prayer. A short time later, widowed by her husband's sudden heart attack, she was asked to assist in the ordination of her son-in-law. Two younger sons are also preparing for the ministry.

Through her husband's work she had watched her

husband developing the skills needed in administering a local parish and later in state conference activities. Now a mature, knowledgeable Christian leader, she is using these skills at the national level as associate secretary for the Council for Lay Life and Work.

Marriage does not detain a man from the immediate exercise of public ministry. A woman may discover, however, that motherhood is not only a ministry but also a unique *preparation* for ministry. Relieved of the necessity of earning her own living, she can often, with self-discipline, find time for the study and prayer which will deepen her life with God. She draws upon her husband's experience just as he draws upon hers. When, after pain and loss, she finds herself alone, she may have more to offer the church than could have been given in a lifetime of public ministry. But two questions keep tugging at my mind: would a husband have lived longer if he could have shared public ministry with his wife and shouldered some of her home responsibility? Apart from her ordination, would those in a position to offer opportunity have thought about her as a potential candidate for national leadership?

Is Ordination Necessary?

But why should the church ordain any woman before it sees what she is going to do? In the above case, the intention of a ministry beyond the home was not apparent for some years. On occasion, however, as in the case of Mrs. Noel Collins, it is obvious from the beginning that a woman has been called to public ministry. At the age of twelve, she had come under the influence of Dr. Mary G. Evans, who had founded Cosmopolitan Community Church on Chicago's south side. "She led me to the Lord," Mrs. Collins says. "For some years it was my privilege to be associated with her in her tremendous work for God." After completing college and some graduate work, Mrs. Collins taught in high school but continued to serve her church as fully as possible. Graduating from Moody Bible Institute, she taught weekday Bible classes and received an evangelist's license. Her husband, a baker, encouraged her. Clearly called into the ministry in 1940, she was ordained by the Community Ministers' Alliance. Now a widow in her early seventies, Mrs. Collins is pastor of Christ Temple Community Church and teaches seventh and eighth grades in the Evangelical Christian School in Chicago.

In an interview by a church paper she was asked whether or not she had ever run into controversy over "woman preachers." She replied, "I never defend my position because, frankly, no set of theological facts can obliterate the absolute, definite, unmistakable call that I received from my Lord." She advises young women never to try to prove their call to other people, adding, "Surely the God who could use a rooster to convict Peter and an ass to halt Balaam will not despise to use even a woman minister."

Because she was serving a church in her own name, it was clear that Mrs. Collins' ordination was indicated. In the case of Charlotte Jones, a minister's wife, however, there was some ambiguity, as her work strictly complemented that of her husband, pastor of very large churches. With academic training far above average and an avid interest in biblical research and archaeology, she had studied fourteen languages, including Ugaritic, Akkadian, Coptic, Greek, Hebrew and some Arabic, the last of which she took at the American University at Cairo. Educated also in art and business, Mrs. Jones prepared church school curriculum materials for the Congregational Publishing House both before and after her marriage. She also wrote books and articles for her own and other denominations. After they moved to the West Coast, her husband faced a year with no director of religious education, so she tackled that job. Under her leadership that year their church school reached an enrollment of eight hundred, with a peak attendance of six hundred. With her husband she attended three assemblies of the World Council of Churches, doing press, radio and television work.

Widowed late in life, Mrs. Jones worked for her doctor's degree at Claremont School of Theology in California, receiving it at the age of seventy-five. Shortly thereafter, she was ordained, a recognition, no doubt, by her church of the ministry to which she had already given her life. But why seek ordination at that late date? She says it was to "continue my husband's work and my own with more official status." It might be added that a married woman can follow her husband into many fields of service without ordination being strictly necessary, but when he is no longer ahead of her, ordination opens the doors. Mrs. Jones also regarded this as an act of more complete consecration. At present, she continues to lecture, preach and write.

Two widows among my respondents are pastors of Friends Churches. In their local groups, Quakers watch for the appearance of gifts of ministry and, upon recognizing them, urge preparation for service. God ordains ministers, Friends believe; the church merely records them. The recording is proposed at the local level but guidance is given and final action is taken by the more inclusive body.

One Quaker widow had gone into the ministry long before her marriage to a businessman, a widower with children. She has completed fifty years of service. The other, a mother of two children, felt called after the death of her husband. She had been active in church school and youth work and, sensing her gifts, the local meeting proposed her recording. She has served twenty years, at the same time teaching in elementary schools. Under her leadership, extensive improvements have been made in church property. (The "nesting instinct" makes women aware of deficiencies in church homes as well as in their private dwellings.) She is devoted to pastoral work and finds no difficulty in counseling either men or women. Since her children are married, she is able to do her calling after school; in case of emergency she calls before school:

> I telephone my principal and let him know I will be there in time for class, but I may be a bit later than we are usually expected in our rooms. It is always quite acceptable with him. In case of funerals my school administrators are willing to get me a substitute.

One cannot picture male clergy in a setting like this. As has been suggested, the ministry of women may develop along lines quite similar to that of men, but again it may not. Perhaps we should weigh the qualifications for ordination on a different set of scales, one which will be considered in the next chapter.

CHAPLAINCIES FOR WOMEN?

Discontinuity of choice has been noted several times as a factor in the maturing of feminine vocation; also noted was the view of many widows that they could not have given time to public ministry while their husbands lived and their children were at home. Instead of combining jobs, some, like Helen Terkelsen, have had two consecutive careers.

Mrs. Terkelsen, wife of a manufacturer, did not enter seminary until her three children were in prep school and college. Her husband, "a fine layman [deacon], approved. Without his cooperation, I couldn't and wouldn't have done it." After receiving the degree of Bachelor of Divinity and Master of Sacred Theology in Pastoral Psychology, she became chaplain in a home for unwed mothers and a home for aged women, continuing in clinical pastoral education until she was a fully qualified chaplain supervisor, accredited by the American Protestant Hospital Association.

Both church and state have a stake in the adequate counseling of unwed mothers. Social workers are well qualified
to help these young women plan for themselves and their
babies, often making unconscious use of Christian insights
while following the methods of their own profession. But
religious problems may emerge with which secular education could not prepare them to cope: a normal sense of
guilt, the feeling of alienation from God and parents, possibly the aching sense of having betrayed their own spiritual
commitments. As we know, illegitimate pregnancy today is
not confined to the disadvantaged, but may occur in any
environment. Moral standards are so confused that young
people find little help in charting their course.

In her book *Counseling the Unwed Mother*,[7] Mrs. Terkelsen points out that even with the most supportive planning, the giving up of a baby can be a dangerous shock. A
chaplain, with both social work and religious training, can
help to make this experience one which will contribute to
the integrating and maturing of personality. Mrs. Terkelsen
believes that many clergy are "natural" chaplains because
they are good pastors; nevertheless, "counseling is somewhat like golf; you do something very unnatural until you
discover how much more effective it is to have a 'pro' to
guide you." No matter how kind and instinctively wise a
Christian leader may be, the skills of the second profession
help.

Mrs. Terkelsen has standing in the American Association
of Pastoral Counselors and is, at the present time, assistant
director (supervisor of counseling) at the United Church
of Christ Pastoral Counseling Center in Middleton, Massachusetts, as well as a supervisor of clinical pastoral education in the Andover Newton Theological Seminary. She
did not enter the ministry to do parish work but has united
a "secular" and "spiritual" ministry, "helping people remove
the stumbling blocks that interfere with a full life in the
church and bringing them into loving relationship with

both God and men. This takes more time than most parish ministers have to give to it today. We know this by the number of people they refer to us."

Mrs. Suzanne Dettmer, graduate of Union Theological Seminary, made a study of "Some Factors Pertaining to the Work of Women Chaplains in Hospitals," as a part of her degree work. She is of the opinion that this may be an interesting field for women to explore. Her study, although limited in scope,[8] was wide enough to mark out certain areas for future investigation. It appears that stereotyped images of the minister, held by patients who are non-church members, confront both men and women chaplains, helping and hindering them in odd ways. For example, unchurched men may respond to a woman chaplain where male clergy would seem threatening; women do not yet convey a clergy image. On the other hand, in cases of extremely serious illness where death may be feared, the patient who desires prayer may think male clergy are on more intimate terms with God. Here the woman chaplain is thwarted rather than helped by the absence of the image.

Most patients seemed open to both men and women chaplains. Many felt it would be desirable if a choice could be offered. It is noteworthy, however, that nearly half of the women preferred a female chaplain and that nearly one-fourth of the men concurred. Nearly one-fourth of the men preferred a male chaplain and one woman concurred. One-third of the men, as compared to one-fifth of the women, saw ability and personality as more important than sex in chaplaincy work. A few of the men who wanted a male chaplain, however, were vigorous in their protest against women in this work, one saying, "No thanks. I cannot see God's image mirrored in a woman." Another remarked that if he were in great pain, he might not "hold his language down" even if the chaplain were a woman. That his doubts were not without justification is disclosed by the experience of a married respondent. Visiting a male hospital ward, early in her training, she met a young fellow who, shaken by bad medical news, blurted out, "I suppose you are here to save my goddamned immortal soul!"

"No," she responded firmly, "I just stopped in to say 'hello'; you can decide about your own soul."

After that, he welcomed her calls and arranged for her to meet his wife.

A PIONEER MINISTRY

Some widowed respondents have found their way into unusual forms of ministry. My questionnaire had asked, "Are there specific phases of ministry in which women can make a distinctive contribution or in which they are inadequate, or do you consider this a question of individual difference unrelated to sex?" Approximately 160 women to whom I first sent the questionnaire responded to this inquiry which had been marked "optional." Of the number, one-third considered qualification for ministry unrelated to sex and made no further comment. Several of those who replied more fully pointed out that women could not act as chaplains in a men's prison, though one observed that nurses serve male wards in hospitals: "What is the difference?" In the variety of answers given, the underlying thought seemed to be that there is no more limitation in the spiritual care women can give to men than vice versa.

Surprisingly, one woman, Mrs. Carol Hyde of Columbus, Ohio, is performing the "impossible" task of working with male ex-convicts. After taking all the relevant courses offered by Oberlin Graduate School of Theology, including six quarters of work in various institutions as trainee, and after serving as chaplain in a center for mentally retarded persons, Mrs. Hyde was called as a counselor to Alvis House. Alvis House is a professional treatment center and temporary home for prisoners rejoining free society. The director, Maurice Breslin, an eleven-year veteran of halfway house experience, looks at it this way: "Men who have been shut up in prison for years, with only men for companions, need to have an exposure to women in the way-station between prison and community." In group therapy sessions there is value in having both male and female attitudes and viewpoints expressed. Well established now, Alvis House hopes to serve from 120 to 150 persons a year in residence as well as to give outpatient service. The staff plans to work especially with young men for whom crime is not yet a fixed way of life.[9]

One part of Mrs. Hyde's work is to visit prisons and interview men who expect to be on parole in the Columbus area, with a view to discovering those most likely to benefit from Alvis House experience. "At first there were some eyebrows raised at the idea of admitting a woman to a male prison for interview purposes," Mrs. Hyde says, "but now there is no problem." She explains that the work is privately funded and adds, "Sometimes the funds are so private you can't see them." But the board looks forward with confidence to enlarged facilities.

The question might well be asked, nevertheless, how the church regards one of its ordained ministers functioning in this fashion. A Unitarian-Universalist, Mrs. Hyde approached the Fellowship Committee of the Ministers' Association with her plan, motivation and goals. They were open to her purpose and recognized that this is indeed a ministry.

The Woman's Pulpit reports that Nora Calvert, a Presbyterian minister, formerly of New Zealand, is now chaplain at Beaumont School for Boys at Richmond, Virginia. Churchmen there felt, too, that a woman's viewpoint would be helpful in counseling youth between fifteen and eighteen years of age who had been in trouble with the law. She works with both individuals and groups, and is also responsible for religious education in the school.[10] It may in time become apparent to most people that gifts and personality are more important than sex in determining an appropriate field in which to work.

Ordained to Ecumenical Mission

Along with service in their own localities, Christian churches face international obligations which, in the last century, have found expression in such organizations as the World Council of Churches. Up to the present time, male clergy have predominated in the guidance and government of this body. When Elsie Thomas Culver was called to the staff of the Division of Church World Service, with one of her responsibilities being to conduct interviews with the clergy of Europe, some thought it wise for her to be ordained. This immediately raised the question as to how such a decision could be related to the understanding of ordination as a setting apart for the ministry of word and sacrament. A California association of the United Church of Christ thought ordination to an ecumenical and writing ministry appropriate and gave her this status in 1944.

Mrs. Culver was well prepared for both the professional and spiritual aspects of her work. She had majored in international law at the University of California and had realized while attending a Quaker-related conference that international relations and religious illiteracy were incompatible. With the thought of auditing courses for a semester, she entered Pacific School of Religion at Berkeley. Fascinated, she stayed and worked for her M. A. and B. D. degrees. The last twenty-five years have been given to ministry beyond the local parish.

But the United Church of Christ, now engaging in the Consultation on Church Union, faces the fact that it has no uniform criteria for ordination; each association makes up its own mind as to what constitutes ministry. The suggestion is being made that the church "might strengthen its mission to the world with a clearer definition of ordination and a stronger sense in the whole church of what this body of (ordained) men and women are up to on its behalf." [11] Would it not be a pity if such ministry were to be so narrowly conceived as to eliminate from professional activity persons who have served the church in such capacities as Mrs. Culver? In addition to her public relations work with the World Council of Churches, she has written a scholarly and sparkling book *Women in the World of Religion.*[12] In 1960, she became founder and executive director of Senior Peace Builders, Inc. Started with the support of elderly professional people who, not content with war, wanted to make a positive contribution to peace, the organization now includes persons of all ages and on all continents. While the slogan, "Push out the borders of the peaceful areas of life," sounds nebulous, a practical mimeographed piece, *The Cornerstone,* nearing a decade of circulation, pools news and views on peace. Mrs. Culver donates her services to this work, which offers a quick way of finding out what is being said and done at many levels.[13]

A LEGACY OF COURAGE

With the trend to increased specialization, in the ministry as elsewhere, many will have only a vague idea of the typical daily program of a minister of Christian education. Constructing a composite picture from our responses, it could be said that her day begins in the church office as she looks over the mail, writes letters, and checks her appointments. If the church has weekday nursery school for average or exceptional children, or a day care center, she will make sure that everything is in order there. Since churches also try to work with other institutions to help youth break out of delinquency patterns, she may be scheduled to attend a Model Cities meeting with representatives of juvenile courts, civic groups, and others, planning a foster home with parents and social worker in residence for half a dozen or more teen-age boys in the hope that institutional correction may be avoided.

Our minister of Christian education may have lunch with a college student adviser who is doing field work in the church and, in the process, is alienating adults through over-identification with the most uninhibited youth. She will try to widen his comprehension of the problem. On the way back to the church she may drop in at the public school to discuss with counselors there possible cooperation in guiding youth for whom they are mutually responsible. The afternoon may be spent in counseling at the church with teachers or superintendents of the various departments who need help with new curriculum materials or in homes where mothers cannot understand the actions and attitudes of their own children. One such minister estimates that three-fourths of her time is spent in counseling. Another says:

> I work with families in this inner city neighborhood. This may include referring them to an agency that can help them or trying to do some listening—if I were bold I would say counseling—with mothers, teens and children. Adults around here are worried and preoccupied.

In the evening, she may be at a church-school teachers' meeting, at the coffee house where college students gather, speaking on some aspect of Christian education to a women's group in an outlying community where the church has only one pastor, working with a sub-committee of the Council of Churches, or attending a play with a friend.

A college chaplaincy represents a specialized ministry of education. A widow in her late forties serves as chaplain at a junior college where she teaches Bible and "a sort of human encounter course." She also plans a service of worship once a week, usually securing outside speakers but occasionally leading it herself. The major part of her time, however, is spent with the students. Sometimes conversations with them are scheduled, but more often they are just "informal happenings."

> In these individual meetings I try to be really present with the student where he is, and to share with him, when he allows me or asks me, my own excitement in the Christian faith. It is my firm belief that we come to know the love of God only as we see love for ourselves expressed by others, even when we are unlovely. So I approach them in this spirit without fanfare, in simplicity, vulnerable to their rejection or acceptance, not imposing religion upon them—just being there in prayer and hope that God will use me in this place for his purposes. It is intangible, frustrating, fatiguing, exciting, fulfilling, rewarding—all of these things.

Ordained in a denomination which has only recently given such recognition to women, she is invited to preach from time to time, but has not yet been asked to administer the sacraments. Facing her situation realistically, she accepts the fact that the pulpit will probably not really welcome women in her fifteen remaining years of active service. She does not want to work on a denominational board, remote from the people. She is, therefore, planning to secure her doctorate in personnel services at a secular institution, so the degree will be recognized in secular educational circles, and to remain in the college milieu.

This woman has been a widow only a few years. Her husband approved her entering seminary and preparing for the ministry. He knew his condition, lived to see her graduate, and died the following summer, a victim of cancer.

She describes her call to the ministry in down-to-earth terms as "no rosy, easy path of perpetual mountaintop experiences or emotional binges," but as the "culmination of a long journey where the destination finally became inevitable." In reading these words, my mind went back to Roman Catholic Sister Madeleva's autobiography *My First Seventy Years*. In 1925, Sister Madeleva faced the three-hour public oral examination for her doctor's degree at the University of California. A Catholic sister, facing such a test then, must have been as frightened as a Protestant woman facing her examination for ordination, and Sister Madeleva uses the same language, "Looking back now, all seems to have moved in quiet, ordered inevitability." A professor told her, "The thing that came through to all of us most clearly was that you were sustained by something beyond mere academic competence." [14]

Catholic sisters and Protestant women ministers have more in common than meets the eye. Obviously, Sister Madeleva was not speaking from a Calvinistic point of view but when a woman, whatever her faith, is willing to move forward, following the initiative of God, "day after unpredictable day," a time often comes when, glancing back, she can observe that decisions made without knowledge of the future have, nevertheless, been shaped to what looks like an all-encompassing divine strategy.

Widows believe that their husbands played a large part in their own unconscious pre-preparation for the ministry. One says:

> I think that marriage, when spiritually rich, has been a training ground for the ultimate relationship of the individual with God. The constancy, forgiveness and understanding in a good marriage prefigure each one's ultimate realization that God's love is all wise and more. Marriage for me was an immense enrichment of my growing "practice of the presence of God."

The widow, whose husband died of cancer, adds, "He left me such a legacy of courage, too."

6.

Why Extend Ordination?

Protestants visualize the minister as a married man who gives "full time" service to the church from a reasonably early age. Sex aside, single women fall short of this image merely because they are single. Married women, it is thought, should not (and often cannot) give full time. Widows have a late start. As a respondent says, "Neither the single ordained woman nor the married career woman fits into the norms of our society."

Why not, then, close the question of ordination for women by ruling it out? The experience reflected in this book has shown that the issue needs closer examination. First, God is calling women to the ministry. We have seen, moreover, that eighty or more churches already ordain them, thus making it possible for the church as a whole to observe and evaluate their efforts. We have posed the problem women present in the way society insists it must be posed, that is, in terms of their relationship to men, their marital status. Challenging this underlying assumption would have meant another kind of book. That women in all three states of life are functioning effectively in work requiring ordination has been set forth at length.

We must now raise the question which may open a Pandora's box: is the clergy image itself due for the kind of change that would give women more than token participation in the ministry? More than ten years ago, Dr. Madeleine Barot said, "I think that in agreeing to include women in its ministry every church implicitly accepts the questioning of the traditional forms of this ministry." [1] Most women marry, acquiring the occupation of homemaker and mother, so that any change radical enough to affect them on a large scale will affect men as well: if women can take years to make their academic preparation for ordination, why not men? If women can serve the church part time, or with special skills, as ordained persons, why should not men be allowed the same privilege? André Dumas sees these implications and states, "The opening of the ministry to women in the church, at a time when the question of half-time work is more and more discussed in the world, could be an important breach in the wall which separates secular life and ecclesiastical life." [2] But what becomes of a clergy class if those in other occupations, or those reaching a decision for the ministry late in life, are to be accepted as candidates for ordination? And is such separation even desirable? What would the disappearance of such a class mean: accelerating disintegration for the church, or a reformation as striking as that of the sixteenth century? This chapter will try to frame a highly tentative answer to such questions.

IS THE CLERGY AN ELITE?

A great many seminary students today are not at all sure that they want to belong to a ministerial elite, or to enjoy special privileges and be addressed as "Reverend." One young woman who does not plan to be ordained says, "I suppose I see ordination as a handicap to ministry because I see 'the cloth' as a way of separating the ministry of the laity from the 'professional ministry'." Some who are now ordained held the same view when they were younger. One speaks of the "distance" that ordination seems to create:

> Even with persons who do not act as though there were a mysterious sanctity to ordained persons, there is still a feeling that the minister will be able to find answers, solve problems, work miracles, and never become tired, discouraged, or feel the need to "let down her hair."

Another says:

> I would rather have felt that ordination made it possible for me to identify more completely with people and their needs rather than the opposite. Being "set apart" with special status can be an obstacle.

Still another mentions a fellow student in seminary

> who does not want to be ordained as he feels this would separate him from the people among whom he will work. Does this say something about the attitude of the laity toward all who are ordained? I do think the whole concept of ordination is coming into question among many of seminary age today—men as well as women.

Another speaks of "occupational isolation." In all these instances the point seems to be that modern society looks upon the clergy as an elite.

Respondents were not out of seminary long, however, before the concrete circumstances of everyday life forced them to take a second look at ordination. They ran into the problem: either I must be a lay person, earn my living through secular work and give what time I can to the church, or I must become ordained and be employed by the church as institution. If they desire to remain lay persons, they face the fact that they have no special authorization from the church; they are on their own. The clergy are popularly regarded, and usually regard themselves, as the ones who speak for the church. From the practical (not theoretical) point of view, then, the choice is either belong to the elite or be classed as an amateur. It is not an easy decision to make.

WHAT CAUSES LAY APATHY?

If the laity are as important to the church as the ordained claim, should they not be given more opportunity to help chart its course? Church leaders, charged with responsibility, hesitate at this point, for biblical reasons, as well as others: a clergy class was beginning to emerge when the later New Testament books were written. Is the hierarchical structure, characteristic of most Christian churches, a part of divine revelation, or is this arrangement, borrowed from the society of an earlier day, open to change?

It is clear that Jesus had a circle of intimate friends to whom he gave intensive teaching. After his death, convinced of his resurrection and filled with the Holy Spirit, this small group (the infant church) grew rapidly. At first, those who had known Jesus well were its natural guides. Later, a widening authorized leadership served two purposes: that of distinguishing authentic Christian teaching from fictional writings that were circulating as early as the second century, and that of structuring the movement to meet practical problems such as extension of the mission and charitable work. No one would have known what to believe without some kind of authority and there was no fully authenticated written form. Apostolic writings were still being passed from church to church, since they had not yet been gathered together. For many centuries the vast majority of Christians were illiterate, dependent upon educated priests and those claiming apostolic succession to lead the way.

This situation continued without serious dispute until the time of the Protestant Reformation, when the Bible became for Protestants the normative authority and the priesthood was superseded by the preaching of the word. Perhaps it is time for an equally radical new reformation which would give laymen, too, a chance to assume leadership of such a nature as to bring about another form of authorized ministry. Everyone must realize that we confront a disquieting apathy among church members which has been growing for a long time. This movement seems to have three especially conspicuous facets.

1. Laymen are no longer illiterate, and clergy share the distinction of advanced education with a great many groups which have no hesitation in disputing their word. Those in other professions smile at the claim of theology to be "queen of the sciences," humoring a dogmatic clergyman as one might humor the man who thinks he is Napoleon—and paying about as much attention to him.

2. One does not have to attend church to hear preaching today—if desired, television and radio can bring it into the home. Books and magazines dealing with the Bible are available in variety to those who desire them. Many Protestants observe Holy Communion infrequently and without the clear motivation that takes Catholics to Mass.[3] Add the relativizing trends in our society, and it can be seen at once why for some persons organized worship is being displaced by private pursuits, even when they do not have any specific intention to abandon religious faith.

We have been frequently told, on Scriptural authority, that we must not "forsake the assembling of ourselves together," that lay participation in worship is needed. But how does the layman participate? He sings hymns that have been chosen for him, or stands while others sing them.

He listens to a minister who has planned the worship in its entirety. If, perchance, his local church uses a more elaborate liturgy with sung responses and litanies, he follows the words put into his mouth through the Order of Worship. Is it any wonder that this passive "participation" in the gathered church offers insignificant competition to the mass media?

3. Church leaders turn accusing eyes upon the seminaries. Why did they not anticipate this state of affairs before lay apathy reached such proportions? What are they doing even now to prepare a ministry capable of coping with it? Traditional subjects are still taught: Bible, ancient languages, history of the Christian faith, systematic and practical theology. It is true that some teach sociology and psychology as related to ministerial functions, and others offer courses in world religions, ideologies and cultures. Nevertheless, despite indications that many seminaries are increasingly alert to the need for changes in theological education, many still accuse them of trying to create the church in their own image rather than to function for its upbuilding. Denominational and educational leaders can marshall arguments for their respective positions. The gap remains between the kind of pastors local churches want and the kind seminaries are preparing. With scant knowledge of the concrete problems faced by the laity, young pastors, under the leadership of professors with little or no experience as ministers of local churches, often want to promote political, economic and social programs which seem to them "the only possible course for Christians," but which, to conservative churchmen, appear idealistic nonsense. Not infrequently there is no mental or spiritual ground on which a meeting between pulpit and pew can take place. The seminary graduate sees himself as an authorized Christian leader and cannot understand why his people fail to fall into step behind him. He wonders why

he cannot arouse them to action, and in some cases he is startled to find that he has incurred their ire.

James I. McCord, president of Princeton Theological Seminary, offers what seems to be an accurate analysis of the predicament:

> Today's threats grow out of a tendency to split theological education into separate and discrete parts, with a part of its function being done in academic isolation and other parts taking place in institutions or agencies. The danger in this tendency is manifest. It could easily reduce theology to abstraction and ministry to pragmatic functionalism.[4]

The same seminary may be graduating men interested in archaeological research, and others who want to push the church into the role of challenging the political power structure. They are seminary graduates, nevertheless, and assumed to be ready, if so moved, to serve a congregation. It has been estimated, however, that nearly half of 1969 seminary graduates will go into work other than the parish ministry.[5] In the event their expectations do not materialize (since some fields are overcrowded), they will be seeking a church to serve. Will they be able to do what is expected of them?

THE MINISTRY OF THE WORD

Theoretically, the preaching of the word should unite minister and congregation in a common and growing faith. The pastor is a product of some church that has aroused his interest in the Christian religion sufficiently to make him want to study further. But he has received a scientific grounding in regard to the Scriptures at seminary. Reared by parents who never heard of such an approach to the Bible, and in local churches where pastors may have had little or no time to keep up with developments, seminarians, groping for answers, are shaken by the onslaught of previously unsuspected theories, questions, and tentative judgments. They begin to think of themselves as a professional class whose duty it is to interpret a vast complex of seething religious thought and to move the congregation out to change society. Few laymen are on this wave length.

If the older layman knows anything at all about the Bible, he probably still thinks of it as the "Word of God"; he can be touched rather easily by the evocation of nostalgic memories of devout persons he has known or admired in the past. Younger people, influenced by the culture, come to church to listen respectfully but critically. They are ready to go along with the minister if he can get through to them and if the direction he is taking sounds reasonable.[6] Most Protestant lay people feel, at least vaguely, that preaching ought to deal with the Bible. Is it not the soil from which, directly or indirectly, Christian values have grown?

Perhaps, however, minister and layman view this soil in different ways. The minister, with his scientific, critical,[7] training, has the attitude of a paleontologist; he is looking for bones (problems), trying to answer questions that lay persons may not be asking, or attacking the ills in our society as the prophets did in theirs. Lay persons, on the other hand, when they invest time in listening to a sermon, want something they can use in their lives. Their approach is that of the farmer, and they look to a crop.

A crop, though, is impossible unless the seed of a higher than human word is received by the minister and, through him, by hearers. Preaching which is merely the exposition of a biblical text, plus pronouncements on public affairs, will leave the layman free to take it or leave it. "Ministry of the word" is a rather ambitious way to describe much of the tentative, essay-type communication that comes from some modern pulpits. The layman may not sharply articulate his criticism but possibly he feels that unless there is some current word from the Lord, preaching is presumption. If there is such a word, the pastor should make it heard with authority. Is this too much to ask? Probably not, but what is involved in making it heard is not as simple as the church member may think.

When "ministry of the word" is used with reference to worship, it doubtless applies both to the written and read word of the Bible, and to the spoken word of the preacher. There is, however, a whole constellation of experience behind the effective sermon. The minister has had years of intellectual preparation. He has many tools for keeping up to date on biblical scholarship. Calling, counseling, working with laymen in various capacities, he comes to know them personally and to love them. He tries to read the significant books that appear in areas affecting their lives. But if his motivation is true to the best in Protestant history, the most critical factor in sermon preparation is his responsiveness to the living word, Christ.[8] In penitence, self-discipline and humility, he seeks to open himself fully to that Spirit who makes Christ continuously present and who, given opportunity to act upon his mind, will place him into the continuity of the prophets and apostles.

His constellation, then, consists on the one hand, of the Bible and human need, which it is his business to know, and, on the other hand, the mystery of the intention of Christ for the coming hour of worship, an intention which he must try to fathom. It is his task to communicate that which cannot be imparted by human knowledge alone but which, with the help of God, he must somehow put into words so that hunger for the holy will spring up in the congregation, together with comprehension of the direction in which to move.[9] When he succeeds, he becomes a sacrament of the living word, a vehicle for meanings known only to God and to individual members of the congregation. People will often say, "You preached that sermon just for me," and the preacher will not know what evokes the remark.

How to do this is not taught in seminary. Both verbal and non-verbal communication are taught. Sensitivity training may be given, but sensitivity to the Holy Spirit is too often taken for granted. It is assumed that the student is learning this in his own experience but, if he fails to do so, the most he can accomplish as a minister is to build up an institution, if he has administrative ability, or attract a following, if he has personal magnetism.

The constellation of experience within which the layman works is different. The known quantities for him are the work he has to do and the people to whom he must relate; the mystery is how he can manage to live the Christian life, given the circumstances he faces. He confronts Christ, not in the area of receiving a sermon, but in finding out what is expected of him in his daily work. At one time, it was regarded as the preacher's responsibility to enlighten and "equip" him. The biblical passage usually quoted in support of this view is Ephesians 4:11–12:

> His "gifts unto men" were varied. Some he made his messengers, some prophets, some preachers of the Gospel; to some he gave the power to guide and teach his people. His gifts were made that Christians might be properly equipped for their service . . .[10]

The minister clarified the general principles of the Christian faith which the layman was to put into operation on his job, but is it not much easier to deduce these general principles from the New Testament than it is to apply them to the many occupations of our complex society? Few ministers can hope to know the depth of the dilemmas facing them in the congregation.

In overemphasizing the minister's role, we have overlooked the fact that the layman is able to do a great deal for himself. The same biblical author cited makes this clear

(Ephesians 6:10ff). He saw that Christians were faced with forces beyond their control [11] that could drive them to despair of being able to serve God in the world. He tells them how to arm themselves. In the First Letter of John, moreover, the followers of Christ are informed that they have a teacher within them,[12] not to make them independent of the Christian community but to incorporate them into its thinking so that they can share its mission.

Perhaps this inner dialogue goes on with everyone to some extent; there is no need to magnify the church unduly. God often teaches by the forming of questions in the mind. Giving attention and trying to answer them honestly may cause growth in self-knowledge. A Christian quite often feels that he is not nearly so good a person as the one who works next to him, and never seems to need the church, but proximity to Christ not only lights up personal deficiency but brings an ever-deepening healing to the personality.

The most immediate need of laymen is to retrieve the Bible, which criticism has locked up in ecclesiastical institutions as securely as chains ever bound it to the pulpit in medieval days. The layman, having lost confidence in his ability to read it with understanding, suffers either from indifference to it or from inferiority in the presence of clergy that makes him feel unqualified for any except the most mediocre work in the church. There are, of course, exceptional laymen not covered by such a generalization. Some persons coming to the New Testament with a sense of need and without undue concern about critical problems are surprised at how often it seems suddenly to come alive.

A woman who had held a responsible post with the YWCA at the time of the Second World War told me of such an experience. Needing strength and wisdom, she and two friends began to make an intensive study of the Gospels. They would read agreed-upon portions through the week in a prayerful way and write down what the passage seemed to be saying to them. They would then meet and exchange their reflections:

Christ came as a real and living presence, pulling me on to new ideas and giving me strength along with my two friends. We trusted and corrected each other in this study. There is a living Spirit between you; you meet on a different basis from anywhere else.

If a layman can meet with a small Bible study group made up of members of his own church, or across denominational lines, each person using a different New Testament translation, the interplay of insight can prove fascinating. It is usually better if the minister does not make a habit of attending such gatherings. He has been a teacher so long that he may find it hard not to assume that role, but the more important consideration is that the passages with special meaning for him may not be directly relevant to the needs of lay persons with different preoccupations; he may actually divert them from what they should be finding out. The minister *is* a teacher when it comes to critical problems, but these are not the primary concern of the groups under discussion and his presence may inhibit freedom of expression. It would be natural for him to serve as a resource person and to meet with the group occasionally. Study groups of this kind can be killed by anyone, lay or clerical, who thinks he has all the answers, forcing everything into rigid doctrinal molds and seeking only to confirm present opinions. An open mind and a humble spirit are essential if one is to glimpse the living word through the Bible.

Persons coming to this new kind of fellowship often experience an urgent desire to enlarge it. Some may want to attend a lay school of theology or, if they like the outdoors, to take their families to summer camps or conferences where all may study, enjoy recreation and have opportunity for informal conversation with other laymen and clergymen. Others take church tours with accompanying lecture courses that carry them onto the frontier of the world's need so that they can learn firsthand what the possibilities of service are. Laymen are in a unique position to bring a fresh and needed perspective to the mission of the church. As I see it, their service to God is a problem not so much of communication in prepared words, such as the minister faces, as of commitment to being with Christ in the world. The word will be taken into the public arena not by ministers telling politicians, economists and those in other occupations what to do, nor by those in other occupations telling the minister what the word is, often confusing it with the United States' way of life, but as all Christians try to learn from Christ, becoming willing to change their thinking and style of life.

As laymen journey along such roads as these, however, the time may come when their hearts begin to "burn within them" [13] and there are messages they feel they must deliver to the church. Hearing, the church becomes aware of their understanding of the Christian faith and of the development of their mission. Why, then, should they not be ordained?

This should be no threat to professionally trained clergy. Theological education is a tool for mission if that is the end for which it is used but so, also, are countless other gifts and opportunities. Special status and privilege for the clergy would no doubt become obsolete, but would not most pastors welcome colleagues with whom they could share their heaviest burdens? There has been growing emphasis upon the need of sabbatical renewal for clergy, one suggestion even being made that a young minister with a growing family needs a year free from pastoral duties after he has served four years; the more common suggestion is after six or seven years.[14] Is such overextension of clergy a divine way of letting us know that the time has come to close the cleavage between them and those among the laity who share their commitment?

Would this mean the end of preaching as a means of communicating the word? It might, or it might not; time would tell. If preachers are no longer needed, will not God cease calling them? With growing education, vital participation of laity and proliferation of new types of ministry, preaching might phase itself out as other forms of communication develop. Whether or not this happens, it seems likely that new ways of being together in worship will become common. Cross-disciplinary dialogue where lay persons could discuss their problems and insights across the lines of differing occupations in a setting of worship might replace the sermon. Conferences might be held, gathering those of similar work in a given area, for intensive consideration of their particular concerns. Young people, visiting whatever consultation attracted them, could orient themselves toward future ministry, and would doubtless move on to plans beyond anything we could imagine now. This would not necessarily mean the end of a professional clergy class; it would, however, end the special spiritual status and exclusive responsibility currently accorded that class. The fact that an individual has competence with regard to religious subjects does not automatically make him a Christian leader; he may, or may not, be following the leadership of Christ in his own life. Those who do follow share a common mission.

THE SACRAMENTS

Where would such an approach lead in terms of the sacraments? Shall we prepare to see them phased out, too? There is always the danger that enthusiasts might advocate such a move, but sacramental worship lies at the heart of the public celebration of the Christian people. This is true whether it be the Catholic Mass or the ideal proclamation of the word among Protestants, many of whom do not observe Holy Communion frequently because they wish to preserve its holy meaning. But corporate worship has been associated with a special building so long that the building itself is popularly called "the church." Might it be time to move the sacraments so that the church can become clearly visible to the world?

The fear of making sacred things common is authentic and deep. Perhaps, however, an increasing love could diminish this fear,[15] even though it is as old as Paul's First Letter to the Corinthians, which, as far as we know, contains the earliest written tradition regarding the Lord's Supper. Paul was afraid of the paganism which was always encroaching upon this young congregation and threatening to destroy its life in Christ. His language was so strong [16] (the danger of eating and drinking damnation to oneself, as the King James Version puts it) that many Christians have shivered with apprehension ever since, lest this sacrament be inadvertently profaned.

Possibly today, though, one should be more disturbed over the dangers lurking about the celebration of Holy Communion in our divided sanctuaries than over the evil that may result from consecration at the hands of those without controlled theological education and proper ordination. Such control can be understood; its purpose is twofold: to bear witness to unity and to create or re-create unity. As presently conceived, the principle seems paradoxical. If unity is understood as institutional oneness, the affirmation would mean that the sacrament bears witness to institutional unity and continually re-creates spiritual unity within that institution. If one recognizes more than one institution as relating itself to Christ as head, however, does this not cause exclusive intra-institutional celebration to divide Christ? Is it not at least as legitimate, if the sacrament be taken outside individual Christian communions, to affirm that it bears witness to that spiritual unity which alone can offer hope of eventual institutional reunion? If God is active in this sacrament at all, it seems to me that it will be what it is whether we define it properly or not. Christ has promised to be with his followers and to share his life with them. Is this promise contingent upon the perfection of their intellectual understanding and performance? It was not this kind of failure with which Paul dealt so sternly, but a failure in love.[17] If it is our intention to be with Christ and to receive his life, it is difficult to see how we could be opposing his purpose.

Any threat to institutional unity, however, is terrifying to those who govern churches because they see chaos ahead which would be no service to love. Does authority in the church itself need re-examination?

BY WHAT AUTHORITY?

The locus of authority has been a bone of contention since the first disciples thought Jesus had a spectacular future and vied for the place of honor at his side. It is still unresolved. Jesus contended unsuccessfully with the problem throughout his ministry and was still face to face with it at death. Washing the disciples' feet at the Last Supper was a penultimate attempt to clarify his meaning, but the church has not heard the message in a way to create ideological renewal in its stance on authority, which is still the central cause of division among Christians, a fact which should lead all churches to rethink their position in depth.

Jesus' teaching regarding servanthood is not questioned by the church, but it is interpreted as being consistent with an institutional structure similar to that of secular establishments. Justification for doing this is paradoxically expressed in such statements as: "the one who exercises authority is really a servant." There is, however, a noteworthy difference between a paradox which can be ironed out so as to make clear that two realms of discourse have been juxtaposed and a paradox which will admit of no such straightening because its terms are irreconcilably opposed.

To illustrate: Jesus said, "He that finds his life shall lose it and he that loses his life for my sake shall find it." Obviously, to the Christian at least, "life" here is used in two different senses, that of enjoyable physical existence which takes no cognizance of spiritual reality, and life of such spiritual quality that it is ready for sacrifice to death if this seems to serve God's purpose. This paradox can be ironed out.

Can a similar procedure be used with a saying like "One who exercises authority serves"? Placed into the form of the paradox discussed above, this statement would read, "He who exercises authority serves but he who serves for my sake exercises authority." Has not the word "authority" undergone the same subtle change in this statement as "life" in the other? It is no longer authority as the secular world understands the term, but the spiritual authority which derives from holy service and is, in fact, the only authority that adult human nature regards as compelling without the use of force. Is not this the kind of authority that Jesus himself exercised? Did he ever authorize the use of any other?

Are we implying, then, that the Christian community must exist as movement rather than as institution? This deduction does not seem necessary if the institution itself can move and prove flexible to the purpose of God, but such capacity is not a noteworthy characteristic of any establishment. Still, the church *could* be different; it *could* show unique characteristics, even as institution, which would suggest to mankind its origin in a mission from God. It is urgent that church leaders give their attention to this. Work to be done calls for organization to which a movement, by its very nature, cannot respond: education which necessitates well-integrated planning, mass communication which requires vast sums of money, coordinated relief of human suffering and many other projects demanding administrative gifts with gradations of responsibility.

It would seem, however, that government in the church should be so related to the Christian community that mission could never be throttled by lack of vision on the part of those at remote ecclesiastical controls. It appears to me that basing ordination upon full Christian commitment and consciousness of mission would itself help to make a more relaxed administration feasible. With the present limited number of clergy and an undifferentiated laity, made up of those representing many levels of loyalty and understanding, it seems obvious that the institutional church needs firm steering by those who clearly discern dangers and opportunities. But as Christians become literate regarding the source-book of their faith and assume active responsibility for ministry on the basis of such literacy, it would seem that the locus of authority might be decentralized so that the varieties of mission in various localities could be understood and guided where they might also be observed and evaluated. Worldwide communication would still be necessary for Christians.

WHAT DOES ORDINATION ACCOMPLISH?

It would further such communication for the church to be able to identify its real ministers. There is no cleavage in fact between fully committed laity and clergy, so the dichotomy between them is false and, it seems to me, should be eradicated. The basis of ordination, then, might be as follows. For churches that practice infant baptism, the progression would be first to confirmation when the young person is sure that he wants to accept the vows his parents have taken on his behalf. He would then be expected to search out through prayer and study the ministry to which he wishes to commit himself. This might or might not take a long time but, when he is willing to place himself fully at the disposal of Christ and can give the church a clear, though far from complete, idea of what he thinks his mission is, he would be ready for ordination. It would thus be not the *function* which is ordainable but the *person*. Churches that hold the doctrine of "believers' baptism" would perhaps dedicate infants at the altar without the use of water; baptism and confirmation would be essentially the same rite; and young people would proceed in the same way toward ordination. No pressure would be put on anyone to be ordained as no special status would be attached to ordination, but those sharing it could be aware of the length and depth of the commitment uniting them. The only laity would be those not yet trusting themselves (ideologically) to the living word and not yet aware of any personal mission. This is not to disparage them but to recognize the many shades of existing church membership.

The identification of a person's ministry is important to self-image. Even Jesus sought acknowledgment of his identity from others: "Who do you say that I am?" Peter's recognition of him as the Christ was the turning point of Jesus' public ministry.

Seminary trained women who have been refused ordination, although they have given years of devoted service, suffer keenly from this lack of identification by the church. One relates her experience in doing the work of a hospital chaplain without the status:

> When I call on patients in the hospitals we serve I am usually taken for a volunteer. I am sure the patients do not have a clear idea of who I am. To try to explain my role is very awkward even if a patient is interested and asks. I am amused when I think of how mystifying it would sound if

I said that I was a certified church worker . . . I would appreciate beyond measure the designation of "chaplain." My ministry would be made infinitely easier. Everybody knows what a chaplain is and the idea of a woman chaplain, although experienced for the first time, is not too bizarre for the majority of persons I visit to comprehend . . . I have had some amusing and frustrating times as a result of my pioneering role as a non-chaplain. I have tried to explain my employment to the Social Security people and to the Internal Revenue. I am not a minister. I am not a licensed practitioner (Christian Science). I am not employed by a church (the chaplaincy pays my stipend). I am not employed by the hospital (although my check comes through a hospital payroll). I seem to be thoroughly out of step with our computerized age and I shudder whenever I have a blank to fill out that asks for "nature of employment." [18]

Is the church failing this woman? Perhaps a respondent from the United Church of Canada would say that it is; she defines call as threefold: "the need, the inner call of God in one's life, and the recognition by the church of that call."

A second accomplishment of ordination is the consecration and empowering of the individual by the church. Alone, we are so small. Our covenants with God often waver and we wonder how secure they are. Ordination places us firmly within the ongoing reality of the church's covenant with God, which is itself based upon the covenant of Israel and the new covenant in Jesus Christ. That does not waver. But does not baptism itself place us into this covenant? I believe it does in a beginning way, but we are free personalities and ordination would be that act in which we give ourselves up *wholly* to be integrated into the church's everlasting covenant with God and to join the mission of Christ. A respondent says that the church entered in a supportive way into the "decision or act which had already taken place between my Lord and me." Another believes, "Ordination has given me the strength to continue working in the church when it would have been easier to make a living in other ways."

Some go even further, referring to the "sign" and "seal" of ordination. A minister of the Wesleyan Church expresses it:

> In the laying on of hands after taking the sacred vows, I sensed by his Spirit the greatness of my privilege and the seriousness of the responsibility that was being placed upon me by his visible church and by him who is its glorious and definite head.

Protestants do not think of Holy Orders as a sacrament but perhaps a closer study of the laying on of hands in the New Testament Church would yield insight. Often this act of the church is accompanied by a transmission of power —healing, confirming, commissioning for mission. This was brought home to me through a rather strange personal experience.

Some years ago, I belonged to a small interdenominational prayer group which met in the home of a Methodist widow. When persons came with a desire for healing or other help, we often prayed with the laying on of hands, sometimes even anointing with oil in the name of Christ.[19] The widow received calls during the day from those requesting prayer without attending. One night we were shocked by her report of a woman who had said, "I don't believe in God; I don't believe in Jesus Christ, but I do believe in your prayers. Will you remember me tonight?"

For a moment we sat stunned and then I said, "What are we doing here? She doesn't believe in God but she believes in us. It makes our gathering seem almost blasphemous." An Episcopal priest had the answer:

She does not believe in God nor in Christ, but she does believe in the Holy Spirit without knowing it. When we gather here to pray in the name of Jesus, we are no longer isolated individuals. We are united, on behalf of people, through the power of the Holy Spirit. She senses that and believes in him.

Perhaps this is what happens at an ordination without our being fully aware of it. The church has gathered; we are no longer isolated individuals; the Holy Spirit is invoked with the laying on of many representative hands; that same Spirit is acting through us to seal another into the holy covenant which passes along through the centuries, unaffected by the coming and going of individual priests and ministers. Should we not all be admitted when ready?

NOTES

PREFACE

1. *Consultation on Church Union* (Cincinnati, Ohio: Forward Movement Publications, 1967), p. 53. It is clear that all ordained clergy who are in good and regular standing in the uniting churches will be made clergy of the united church through the act of unification. The words, "God calls men," are not intended to rule out women; my point is simply the ambiguity of the words as they stand.

2. The Episcopal Church is a member of the Consultation on Church Union.

3. Benson Y. Landis, *Religion in the United States* (New York: Barnes and Noble, 1965). The figures are quoted by Elsie Thomas Culver, *Women in the World of Religion* (Garden City, New York: Doubleday & Company, Inc., 1967), p. 218. Other churches have recently decided to extend ordination to women.

I. THE DEVELOPING MINISTRY OF WOMEN

1. See also Matt. 9:18–26; Luke 8:40–56.
2. Mark 8:22–26.
3. Mark 15:40–1; Matt. 27:55–6; Luke 23:49.
4. Luke 10:1–23.
5. John 11.
6. Matt. 19:2–9; 10:2–13.

7. Luke 24:11.

8. M. Madeline Southard, *The Attitude of Jesus Toward Woman* (New York: George H. Doran Company, 1927), p. 137ff.

9. S. MacLean Gilmour, "The Gospel According to Luke," *The Interpreter's Bible* VIII (New York: Abingdon-Cokesbury Press, 1952), pp. 8–9. Note point 3.

10. The Holy Spirit in the New Testament seems sometimes to denote a divine Person and at other times a powerful influence.

11. H. T. Andrews, "Hebrews: Introduction," *The Abingdon Bible Commentary* (New York: The Abingdon Press, 1929), p. 1297. New Testament references to Priscilla (Prisca): Acts 18: 2, 18, 26; Romans 16:3; I Cor. 16:19; and II Tim. 4:19.

12. W. Sanday and A. C. Headlam, "The Epistle to the Romans," *The International Critical Commentary to the Holy Scriptures of the Old and New Testaments* (New York: Charles Scribner's Sons, 1895), p. 422.

13. *Ibid.*, p. 423.

14. Acts 16:14, 40.

15. M. H. Shepherd, Jr., "Prophet in the NT," *The Interpreter's Dictionary of the Bible* (New York: Abingdon Press, 1962), pp. 919–20.

16. Acts 21:9.

17. Scholarly opinion differs as to the identity of these people: were they Greek-speaking Jews, Jews who had adopted Greek customs, or actually Greeks? See the discussion in *The Interpreter's Bible* IX, *op. cit.*, p. 88.

18. Elsie Thomas Culver, *op. cit.*, pp. 70–1.

19. Edith Deen, *Great Women of the Christian Faith* (New York: Harper & Brothers, 1959). For her story, see pp. 34–7.

20. Frances Parkinson Keyes, *Three Ways of Love* (New York: Hawthorn Books, 1963), p. 246.

21. Deen, *op. cit.*, p. 58.

22. B. Forshaw, "Doctor of the Church," *The New Catholic Encyclopedia* IV (New York: McGraw-Hill Book Company, 1967), p. 939.

23. The complicated, but fascinating, question regarding marriage as a sacrament is discussed by E. Schillebeeckx, O. P., *Marriage: Human Reality and Saving Mystery* (New York: Sheed & Ward, 1965), p. 280ff.

24. I Cor. 7:1, 7–10, 25ff.

25. Deen, *op. cit.*, pp. 108–16; Culver, *op. cit.*, p. 144. For an extensive study of Anne Hutchinson and the period, see Emery

Battis, *Saints and Sectaries* (Chapel Hill: The University of North Carolina Press—published for the Institute of Early American History and Culture, 1962).

26. Helen Augur, *An American Jezebel* (New York: Brentano's, 1930), p. 272.

27. Constance M. Coltman, "Post-Reformation: The Free Churches," in A. Maude Royden's book, *The Church and Woman* (London: James Clarke & Co. Ltd., no date), pp. 112–13.

28. For details concerning the faculty's dilemma over Antoinette Brown, I am indebted to the late Mary H. Candy's thesis. Her source: *Oberlin Alumni Magazine* for April 1920, pp. 153–54.

29. Deen, *op. cit.*, p. 395.

30. Deen, *op. cit.*, p. 396. Antoinette Brown married into a remarkable family, the Blackwells. One sister-in-law was the first woman doctor of medicine in the U. S. in the modern era; another founded the first hospital for women in New York City. In 1859, women doctors were having a difficult time also. Cf. Anna Garlin Spencer, "Woman's Share in Social Culture" (1912), in *Up from the Pedestal*, ed. by Aileen S. Kraditor (Chicago: Quadrangle Books, 1968), p. 103. This volume also contains an address (1873) by Antoinette Brown Blackwell, "Relation of Woman's Work in the Household to Work Outside," pp. 151–59. See also Laura Kerr's biographical novel, *Lady in the Pulpit* (New York: Woman's Press, 1951).

31. *Annual Register* for the 56th year, Hartford Theological Seminary, 1890.

32. Lydia Sanderson Capen, *Historical Sketch of the Woman's Board of the Hartford Theological Seminary* 1889–1939, printed by the Woman's Board, 1939, p. 16.

33. Nine other women stated they had changed denominations in the interest of wider ministry without mentioning the one to which they had first belonged.

34. "A Denominational Executive Comments," *Information Service*, published by the Central Department of Research and Survey, National Council of Churches, Vol. XXXIII, No. 10, March 6, 1954.

35. Thomas Alfred Tripp, "Professional Standards of Women Ministers," *The Minister's Quarterly*, Vol. V, No. 3, August 1949.

36. Candy, *op. cit.*, p. 64.

37. Margaret J. Roxburgh, 29 Thurloe Court, Fulham Road, London S. W. 3, England, Chairman of the Anglican Group for the Ordination of Women to the Historic Ministry of the Church

(of which the president is The Lord Bishop of Birmingham), wrote the history, *Women's Work in the Church of England,* 1958.

38. This study, published August 1968, may be obtained from the Church Information Office, Church House, Westminster, S. W. 1, London, England. See p. 39.

39. For a brief account, see Culver, *op. cit.,* p. 219.

40. Information relative to the Lutheran Council was given in a personal letter from Paul D. Opsahl, Assistant Executive Secretary, Lutheran Council in the U. S. A.

41. R. Lauer, "Feminism," *The New Catholic Encyclopedia* V, *op. cit.,* p. 882.

42. Mrs. Catherine McCarthy, "Woman's Role in the Church," *The Woman's Pulpit,* Vol. 45, No. 2, April–June 1967, p. 7. (Reprinted by permission from *Information Directors Newsletter,* Bureau of Information, National Catholic Welfare Conference.)

43. *Ibid.*

44. Rosemary Lauer, "Women Clergy for Rome," *The Christian Century,* Vol. LXXXIII, No. 37, September 14, 1966, pp. 1107–10.

45. Ruud J. Bunnik, *Priests for Tomorrow* (New York: Holt, Rinehart and Winston, 1969), pp. 137–45; 208–09. See also R. Van Eyden's statement, "If the fundamental dignity of being a Christian is given to men and women without distinction, one fails to see why the functional dignity of the Church's ministry should be denied to female Christians." "Women in the Church's Ministry: A Dutch Report," *Journal of Ecumenical Studies,* Vol. 5, No. 4, Fall 1968, p. 829.

46. Lauer, *op. cit.* Interesting trends may be noted, also, in Sally Cunneen's *Sex: Female Religion: Catholic* (New York: Holt, Rinehart and Winston, 1968), chapter 9.

47. "Progress Report to the House of Bishops from The Committee to Study the Proper Place of Women in the Church's Ministry," October 1966, p. III. (The Bishop of Rochester is chairman of this committee.)

48. Two Orthodox statements appear in *Concerning the Ordination of Women,* Department of Faith and Order, World Council of Churches, Geneva, 1964.

2. A SENSE OF MISSION

1. Martin Heidegger, *What Is Called Thinking?* A translation of *Was Heisst Denken?* By Fred D. Wieck and J. Glenn Gray (New York: Harper & Row, 1968), p. 142.

2. Trudi Klijn, " 'Proper' in the Pulpit," *Response* (United Methodist Women), Vol. I, No. 3, March 1969, p. 12.

3. Adele Spencer, "Women Who Minister," *Concern* (Presbyterian), April 1968, pp. 21–2.

4. Lotte Bailyn, "Psychology of Professional Women," *Daedalus*, Vol. 93, No. 2, Spring 1964, p. 707. The issue deals with "The Woman in America."

5. Disturbed at an early age by uprushes from the unconscious, Jung seems to have been greatly puzzled, at first, as to their message or interpretation. Early religious training, in conflict with intellectual development, doubtless contributed to his distress.

6. Dābhār occurs frequently in the Old Testament, perhaps the clearest interpretation of its meaning being Isaiah 55:11.

3. THE MINISTRY OF SINGLE WOMEN

1. A description of opportunities is given by Benson Y. Landis, *Careers of Service in the Church* (New York: J. B. Lippincott Co., 1964).

2. Marie E. Hubbel, "What Is It Like to Be a Woman Minister?" *Monday Morning*, January 29, 1968.

3. Because this passage contradicts I Corinthians 11:5 and 13 and because it appears at the end of the chapter in some early manuscripts, many commentators are of the opinion that it was added by a later editor who, believing I Timothy 2:11–12 to have been written by Paul, incorporated it here. Few scholars today believe that I Timothy was the work of Paul.

My own view is that Paul remained ambivalent on the question of female freedom. When women used their liberty with intelligence, he did not suggest curtailing their activity, but when they brought criticism upon the church, he remembered the prohibitions of his early training. Many passages in his writings, however, make it clear that for him Christ superseded the law and abolished all privilege based on race, class or sex.

4. Galatians 3:28.

5. This incident is related in *The Woman's Pulpit*, Vol. 46, No. 4, October–December 1968, p. 4.

4. THE MINISTRY OF MARRIED WOMEN

1. All other respondents, listed in Appendix 2, have answered directly.

2. The conference reading program is explained more fully in Chapter 5.

3. It is desirable to have the closing service of Holy Communion led by a participant in the retreat. Male clergy, coming to conduct this one period of worship, are at a disadvantage because they do not know what insights have emerged and hence cannot integrate them into the high moment of self-giving and consecration.

4. William Douglas, *Ministers' Wives* (New York: Harper & Row, 1965). This study gives the results of a questionnaire to which 6,000 ministers' wives from 37 denominations responded. More than a fourth of these women felt that they had been called to be ministers' wives.

5. Flora Slosson Wuellner, *Prayer and the Living Christ* (Nashville: Abingdon Press, 1969).

6. A charge is a parish assignment which may include one or more churches.

7. Many books have been written by ministers to help people meet grief and mourning. Mrs. Faust has prepared a small book in which doctors share their experience. It is entitled *The Light Still Shines*.

8. An association is a regional grouping of churches. It may cover a large or small geographical area, depending on the concentration of churches in a given locality. In this instance there is dense concentration of churches and the second association mentioned was also near the respondent's home.

9. Romans 11:29.

10. A larger parish may be formed where several churches decide to work as segments of one large unit, sharing staff, materials, training sessions for laity, etc. Usually a multiple staff is possible. The respondent is the only coordinator for the three small churches, enabling them to have regular ministerial service and a unified program for the whole community in which each church helps the others with special projects.

11. An A. B. degree is a prerequisite for the degree of Bachelor of Divinity.

12. There are several ways of understanding what constitutes ministry.

13. The view that ministers should not have special friends among the laity is widely held. It is hard to see how any human being can avoid finding some persons more congenial than others. Perhaps the important thing is not to give special public attention to one's friends but to seek out (and encourage loyal lay people

to seek out) the newcomers, the lonely, the unloved or the disturbed. If parishioners observe too close a relationship between pastor and a favored few in the congregation, they may be reluctant to share confidences for fear they might be inadvertently revealed.

14. This article, subtitled "Evidence from Research," appeared in *Child Development*, Vol. XXXI, 1960, pp. 749–82. Note p. 779.

15. Gregory Baum, "Where Is Theology Going?" *The Ecumenist*, Vol. 7, No. 3, March–April, 1969, p. 34.

5. THE MINISTRY OF WIDOWS

1. Hilda Libby Ives, *All in One Day* (Portland, Maine: The Bond Wheelwright Company, 1955), p. 32. Mrs. Ives, United Church of Christ minister, died in December 1969.

2. *Ibid.*, p. 54.

3. *Ibid.*, p. 71. This is a highly original rendering of Matt. 24:28.

4. Margaret E. Henrichsen, *Seven Steeples* (New York: Harper & Row ChapelBook Edition, 1967), p. 3.

5. *Ibid.*, p. 137.

6. *Ibid.*, p. 139.

7. Helen E. Terkelsen, *Counseling the Unwed Mother* (Englewood Cliffs, N. J.: Prentice-Hall, Inc., 1964). This book belongs to the Successful Pastoral Counseling Series of which Russell L. Dicks is General Editor.

8. Mrs. Dettmer was assisted in this study by the Reverend Greta Snider, hospital chaplain in Cambridge, Massachusetts, and by a fellow student. Patients in two New York City hospitals received questionnaires but returns from one were not adequate for use in compiling results. The part of the study to which I refer is based on responses of 39 women and 31 men.

9. Bob Waldron, "Help for the Freed Convict," *The Columbus Dispatch Magazine*, November 3, 1968, pp. 8–10.

10. "Boys' School Has a Woman Chaplain," *The Woman's Pulpit*, Vol. 47, No. 2, April–June 1969, p. 5.

11. Gaylord B. Noyce, "Ordained to What?" *United Church Herald*, Vol. 12, No. 6, June 1969, p. 46.

12. This book has been cited frequently.

13. Harriet Kurtz, a married woman respondent in New York, graduate of Union Theological Seminary, was ordained in 1964, as a Commissioned Missionary of the United Church Board for Homeland Ministries, to an experimental ministry represented

by her work in the Citizens' Committee for Global Safety. She and her husband, a layman and World War II Air Force lieutenant colonel, are trying together to mobilize secular as well as religious concern for peace.

14. Sister M. Madeleva, C. S. C., *My First Seventy Years* (New York: The Macmillan Company, 1959), p. 54.

6. WHY EXTEND ORDINATION?

1. Madeleine Barot, "Women and the Ministry," *Laity*, July 1960, No. 9. Dr. Barot does not regard ministries as divisible into those appropriate for men and those appropriate for women, but believes women should be given enough freedom and surrounded with enough confidence to be creative, so that they need not be limited to imitation of men.

2. André Dumas, "Women's Accession to the Pastoral Ministry," *Ministry* A Quarterly Theological Review for Africa, Vol. 8, No. 1, January 1968.

3. I refer to the Roman Catholic belief in the "real presence" and to the persistently strong emphasis upon the crucial importance of attending public worship.

4. James I. McCord, "Our Theological Responsibility," *Encounter*, Vol. 30, No. 1, Winter 1969, p. 24.

5. Gaylord B. Noyce, *op. cit.*, p. 46. "They will go to work in classrooms and denominational offices, in civil rights organizations, in anti-poverty programs, college personnel services and administration."

6. "Death of God" approaches did not sound reasonable. One layman remarked, "Don't these men know that if they once sell us their views, our response will be, 'To hell with the church?'"

7. Occasionally lay persons misunderstand what is meant by biblical criticism because the word "criticism" itself has two almost opposite meanings. It may mean thorough study in order to understand and appreciate, or it may mean censuring. Biblical criticism quite naturally refers to the positive meaning.

8. Sometimes the reference to Christ as the word is called a hellenization of Christianity. In one sense this is true. The Greek *logos*, translated "word," is used in a theological or philosophical sense in the Fourth Gospel but the purpose of "word" is to communicate, and it was among the Jews that Jesus first communicated a new awareness of God.

9. The organization, World Neighbors, grew out of a single

sermon, preached by John Peters in St. Luke's Methodist Church, Oklahoma City.

10. J. B. Phillips, *The New Testament in Modern English* (New York: The Macmillan Company, 1958), p. 415.

11. Paul's interpretation of these "forces" differs from the twentieth century interpretation but the sense of futility apart from the grace of God is the same. For a clear explanation of this passage, see *The Interpreter's Bible* X (New York: Abingdon-Cokesbury Press, 1953), p. 736ff. The work on Ephesians was done by Francis W. Beare and Theodore O. Wedel. See also *The Interpreter's Dictionary of the Bible* A–D, "Armor of God," by Paul S. Minear (New York: Abingdon Press, 1962), pp. 227–28.

12. I John 2:27. Note *Good News for Modern Men* translation (New York: American Bible Society, 1966), p. 532.

13. This is a common way of referring to encounter with the risen Christ. See Luke 24:13ff., especially in *Good News for Modern Men, op. cit.,* pp. 208–09. John Wesley referred to a similar experience, saying his heart was "strangely warmed."

14. "Sabbatical Renewal," *The British Weekly and Christian World* Congregational Edition, London, April 3, 1969, p. 2.

15. I John 4:17–19.

16. I Cor. 11:17–34; note especially verse 29.

17. William Barclay, *The Lord's Supper* (Naperville, Ill.: SCM Book Club, 1967), p. 109. Dr. Barclay (University of Glasgow) calls attention to the fact that I Cor. 11:29 speaks of "the body" as in the Revised Standard Version of the Bible rather than of "the Lord's body" as in the King James Version. He insists, in consideration of the context, that "body" refers to Christians, who constitute "the body of Christ." There is disagreement among scholars, some of them feeling that "Lord's" is here by implication though manuscript evidence is strong for omission from the text.

18. Julia Sibley, "Women Who Minister," *Concern* (Presbyterian), April 1968, p. 20.

19. This is an unusual practice among Protestants. Most persons in the group belonged to the Order of St. Luke the Physician, which originated in the Episcopal Church but has many members of other denominations.

APPENDIX I

QUESTIONNAIRE—ORDAINED WOMEN

Name _____

Address _____

Approximate age: under 40 _____ 40–60 _____ over 60 _____

Seminary attended _____ When ordained _____

Denomination _____

Are you unmarried _____ Married _____ Children _____

Widowed _____   Divorced _____

Work of husband _____

Your present work _____

Please answer the following questions consecutively, beginning after the last question:

1. (a) Why did you go into the ministry? (b) Why did you choose to be ordained? Please answer a, b, or both.

2. In what forms of ministry have you engaged (general parish, educational, institutional, etc.)?

3. Did you find it necessary to change your church (denomination) in order to receive ordination or to receive it with less difficulty?

4. What major obstacles, or special problems, have you encountered prior to or following your ordination (family, parish or community, ecclesiastical)? Did other women and men encourage or discourage you?

5. What are the advantages and disadvantages of marriage and single life in the work of the ministry?

6. If you have time, will you comment on the following questions:
   (a) Have there been significant changes in your theological or general outlook since ordination?
   (b) Are there specific phases of ministry in which women can make a distinctive contribution or in which they are inadequate, or do you consider this a question of individual difference unrelated to sex?
   (c) If married, how do you divide your time among homemaking, professional duties, study and recreation in an average week? What attitude do your children have toward your work?

APPENDIX 2

ORDAINED RESPONDENTS

Miriam Higgins Ackor
Helen Adams
Delila Ann Ahlf
Sylvia E. Aldrich *
Carol Jane Allen
Wilma Allen
Leila W. Anderson
Marlowe Addy Anderson
Helen A. Archibald
Allora Bowman Arnold
Elizabeth H. Baker
Myrtle I. Baker
Mrs. Lt. W. A. Bamford
Julia M. Barber
Mary Ann Barchers
Elsie I. Barrows *
Frances Pratt Bartter
Ruth Sergeant Bast

Lavon Ann Bayler
Doris Belcher
Phyllis Louise Benner
Mary E. Bennett
Alicia R. Bishop
Betty Lindsay Blanton
Frances W. Blumenfeld
Elizabeth A. Bogert
Joan J. Bott
Janet Hartzell Bowering
Clarice M. Bowman
Constance Bradshaw
Linda B. Brebner
Arden Brock
Dorothea Widger Brooks
Rachel Gleason Brooks

Elizabeth C. Brown
Bernice A. Buehler
Emma P. Burrell
Mary H. Candy *
Faith A. Chandler
Ruthanne K. Cochran
Judith Coleman
Noel Virginia Collins
Mildred I. Converse
Merle C. Cook
Emily Warfield Craig
Nancy Jo Crocker
Elsie Thomas Culver
Bernice C. Dalrymple
Elsie Davies
Noemí Díaz
Rhoda Jane Dickinson

* Deceased since study began.

Jean A. Dimond
Mrs. Maj. Bernard
Ditmer
Louise H. Drake
Evelyn M. Duke
Mrs. Richard M.
Eakin
Ruth Eastburg
Eleanor Seaton
Ebersole
Mrs. Robert L.
Edwards
Elizabeth Etz
Ruth Grimes
Ewing
Louise H. Farrior
Dorothy Faust
Ida M. Folsom
Hazel E. Foster
Maj. Mildred G.
Fox
Marion C. Frenyear
Margaret L.
Frerichs
Helen MacRobert
Galazka
Barbara B. Gardner
Wilma C. Geeding
Lois E. Glenn
Eleanor E. Gordon
Barbara Graymont
Mrs. Capt. Gary
Gregg
Esther E. Grether
Evelyn Staples
Grindle
Ruth Grob
Mildred Board
Grubbs
Catherine L.
Gunsalus
Sue Hainey
Gretchen H. Hall

Norma Hall
Helen M. Handley
Bertha A. Hardy
Elva Hardy
Treasie Hardy
Georgia Harkness
Mary Ellen
Harrison
Lois Joy Hartung
Vivian L. Harvey
Marjorie M.
Hawkins
D. Janet Hays
Carrie M. Hazzard
Louise Robinson
Heath
Hazel E. Heffren
Rachel Henderlite
Margaret E.
Henrichsen
Helen L. Herbrecht
Mary Hiatt
Jessie Mae Hicks
Anne Hall Higgins
Nancy Fickett
Hildonen
Elizabeth L. Hill
Charlotte Sue
Holland
Louraine L.
Holsinger
Ruby Walker Holz
Ida Van Dyck
Hordines
Charlotte Mary
HoTopp
Betty L. Howard
Marie E. Hubbel
Uverna Hubbell
Karen E. Huff
Lenore Harris
Hughes
Carol E. Hyde

Mrs. Bernard C.
Ikeler
Phyllis K. Ingram
Ruth Isaacs
Hilda L. Ives *
Laura Lane
Johanson
Elsie A. Johns
Marian Mann
Johnson
Charlotte Chambers
Jones
Norma Ramsay
Jones
Lena A. Keans
Carolyn Kratz
Kissinger *
Bertha Kistler
Ruth Montgomery
Kivette
Olga H. Klepper
Dorothy A. Kling
Helen June Heath
Knapp
Gertrude M.
Knight
Eunice E. Knox
Violet A.
Kochendoerfer
Virginia Kreyer
Martha B. Kriebel
Harriet B. Kurtz
Nellie Lane
Mary Ellen LaRue
Dorothy Lawson
Marjorie Newlin
Leaming
Cecelia C. Learn
Murdale C. Leysath
Marjorie Harjes
Likins
Gertrude V.
Lindener

Verna Lowell
Mrs. Harold L.
  Lunger
Helen Dearborn
  Lyman
Mary Ely Lyman
Julia Anna Macon
Louise Hurd
  MacLean
Mary MacNicholl
Mrs. Edward
  Malzer
Marietta Mansfield
Joyce L. Manson
Elaine Marsh
Elsa Marsland
Mrs. Clarence F.
  McCall
Elizabeth McCort
Elaine McCullough
Jeanette
  McGlinchey
Elizabeth McGuffie
Cullene Evelyn
  McKechnie
Alice Jean
  McMillen
Judy L. Mead
Mrs. Clinton B.
  Meininger
Margaret A.
  Messer
Jacqueline Doherty
  Mills
Wilma Moon
Olah B. Moore
Margaret M.
  Morton
Ethelyn Murray
Mary *Murray*
  Sherman
Cathleen R.
  Narowitz

Tilda *Norberg*
  McClain
Viola Norman
L. Calista Olds
Muriel Olson
Anneliese Opitz
Wilhelmina Payne
Dorothy W. Pease
Gertrude F.
  Peatfield
Dorothy V. Phillips
Mrs. Brig. L.
  Pickering
Mildred L. Pickup
Dora E. Pierce
Emilie P. Pitcock
Carol Rose Polivka
Frances E. Porter
Ruth Powell
Jeanne Audrey
  Powers
Emily B. Preston
Imogene Quinn
Nellie Mae Rector
Catherine Reed
Lois E. Richardson
Doris Kinsley
  Rikert
Clara Maye Rippel
Patricia R.
  Robbennolt
Ruth E. Rogers
Hazel A. Roper
Wilmina M.
  Rowland
Helen L. Royce
E. Janet Rugg
Marilynn Rushton
Letty M. Russell
Mary Hoffman
  Ryan
Mabel Lewis
  Sahakian

Phyllis E. St. Louis
Dorothy Sallee
Lourinda R.
  Sanford
Norma Schlobohm
Charlotte M. Scott
Ruth Mary Shaak
Eunice B. Shaw
Mary Jane Shaw
Geraldine Erma
  Shawda
Jean Kelso Sherman
Mrs. Bradley
  Skinner
Mildred Slack
Anne Pearse
  Smith
Joyce Harkleroad
  Smith
Mildred T.
  Smuland
Greta W. Snider
Adele B. Spencer
Dorothy T. Spoerl
Helen F. Stark
Alma E. Stepanek
Marion Faye
  Stickney
Irene C. Stock
Doris N. Stone
Martha S. Stone
Ella-Jean Streeter
Johanna W.
  Stroetker
Helen Kelsea
  Swarth
Alice Tan-Ditter
Divina del Carmen
  Tapaya
Marian K. Tate
Elsie B. Taylor
Diane Tennis
Helen E. Terkelsen

Mary Pauline
  Thames
Mary Frances
  Thelen
Helen Thomas
Hazel Thompson
Ruth E. Thompson
Lucille M.
  Toothaker
Margaret E.
  Towner
Beatrice Townsend
Emma Justes Trout

Barbara B. Troxell
Almeda C. Vickery
Marideen J.
  Visscher
Esther Vodola
Irma F. Warfield
Lorena J. Warford
Anita Adams
  Watson
Peggy Ann Way
Carolyn P.
  Welch
Bertha White

Mae Daisy
  Whitehead
Eleanor Wilson
Grace M. Wilson
Clara Wood
E. Loleta Wood
Flora Wuellner
Lorna L.
  Wyttenbach
Margaret Yingling
Gladys Doughty
  York
Esther Young

APPENDIX 3

AMERICAN ASSOCIATION OF
WOMEN MINISTERS

The American Association of Women Ministers was formed in 1919 under the leadership of Miss M. Madeline Southard and Mrs. Ella L. Kroft, both Methodists. An article by Miss Southard, appearing in a 1923 issue of *The Woman's Pulpit*, says:

> The original purpose of our association was to bring women who preach into fellowship with each other . . . Another purpose that developed as we planned and prayed was to secure equal opportunity for women in the ecclesiastical world . . . The third purpose, as stated in our constitution, is to encourage young women whom God has called to preach.

This group, including women of sixteen denominations with "others applying," refused to impose rigid doctrinal or educational tests for membership, although a large proportion of its women were college graduates, some with master's and doctor's degrees. They also refused to make distinctions based on race.

The association has an annual assembly and publishes *The Woman's Pulpit* quarterly, filed in Radcliffe College Library. Each year it includes a report on the "Ecclesiastical Status of Women" by Dr. Hazel E. Foster.

The association maintains contact with women ministers in England, Scotland, Germany and Scandinavia, and is contemplating changing its name from American to International Association of Women Ministers.